GREAT ACHIEVERS
LIVES OF THE PHYSICALLY CHALLENGED

Ray Charles

VOICE OF SOUL

David Ritz

Chelsea House Publishers

New York • Philadelphia

CHELSEA HOUSE PUBLISHERS

EDITORIAL DIRECTOR   Richard Rennert
EXECUTIVE MANAGING EDITOR   Karyn Gullen Browne
COPY CHIEF   Robin James
PICTURE EDITOR   Adrian G. Allen
ART DIRECTOR   Robert Mitchell
MANUFACTURING DIRECTOR   Gerald Levine

GREAT ACHIEVERS: LIVES OF THE PHYSICALLY CHALLENGED

SENIOR EDITOR   Kathy Kuhtz Campbell
SERIES DESIGN   Basia Niemczyc

Staff for **RAY CHARLES**
COPY EDITOR   Catherine Iannone
EDITORIAL ASSISTANT   Kelsey Goss
PICTURE RESEARCHER   Wendy P. Wills
DESIGN ASSISTANT   Catherine Ho
COVER ILLUSTRATION   Richard Leonard

Copyright © 1994 by Chelsea House Publishers, a division of Main Line Book Co.
All rights reserved. Printed and bound in the United States of America.

First Printing

1 3 5 7 9 8 6 4 2

Library of Congress Cataloging-in-Publication Data

Ritz, David.
Ray Charles / David Ritz.
p. cm.— (Great achievers)
Includes bibliographical references and index.
ISBN 0-7910-2080-0.
    0-7910-2093-2 (pbk.)
1. Charles, Ray, 1930– —Juvenile literature. 2. Singers—United States—Biogra-
phy—Juvenile literature. [1. Charles, Ray, 1930– . 2. Singers. 3. Afro-Americans—
Biography. 4. Blind. 5. Physically handicapped.] I. Title. II. Series: Great achievers
(Chelsea House Publishers)
ML3930.C443R6 1994   93-30224
782.42164'092—dc20   CIP
[B]   AC MN

CONTENTS

GREAT ACHIEVERS

LIVES OF THE PHYSICALLY CHALLENGED

JIM ABBOTT
baseball star

LUDWIG VAN BEETHOVEN
composer

LOUIS BRAILLE
inventor

CHRIS BURKE
actor

JULIUS CAESAR
Roman emperor

ROY CAMPANELLA
baseball star

RAY CHARLES
musician

ROBERT DOLE
politician

STEPHEN HAWKING
physicist

HELEN KELLER
humanitarian

JACKIE JOYNER-KERSEE
champion athlete

RON KOVIC
antiwar activist

MARIO LEMIEUX
ice hockey star

MARLEE MATLIN
actress

JOHN MILTON
poet

MARY TYLER MOORE
actress

FLANNERY O'CONNOR
author

ITZHAK PERLMAN
violinist

FRANKLIN D. ROOSEVELT
U.S. president

HENRI DE TOULOUSE-LAUTREC
artist

STEVIE WONDER
musician

A Message for Everyone

Jerry Lewis

Just 44 years ago—when I was the ripe old age of 23—an incredible stroke of fate rocketed me to overnight stardom as an entertainer. After the initial shock wore off, I began to have a very strong feeling that, in return for all life had given me, I must find a way of giving something back. At just that moment, a deeply moving experience in my personal life persuaded me to take up the leadership of a fledgling battle to defeat a then little-known group of diseases called muscular dystrophy, as well as other related neuromuscular diseases—all of which are disabling and, in the worst cases, cut life short.

In 1950, when the Muscular Dystrophy Association (MDA)—of which I am national chairman—was established, physical disability was looked on as a matter of shame. Franklin Roosevelt, who guided America through World War II from a wheelchair, and Harold Russell, the World War II hero who lost both hands in battle, then became an Academy Award–winning movie star and chairman of the President's Committee on Employment of the Handicapped, were the exceptions. One of the reasons that muscular dystrophy and related diseases were so little known was that people who had been disabled by them were hidden at home, away from the pity and discomfort with which they were generally regarded by society. As I got to know and began working with people who have disabilities, I quickly learned what a tragic mistake this perception was. And my determination to correct this terrible problem soon became as great as my commitment to see disabling neuromuscular diseases wiped from the face of the earth.

I have long wondered why it never occurs to us, as we experience the knee-jerk inclination to feel sorry for people who are physically disabled, that lives such as those led by President Roosevelt, Harold Russell, and all of the extraordinary people profiled in this Great Achievers series demonstrate unmistakably how wrong we are. Physical disability need not be something that blights life and destroys opportunity for personal fulfillment and accomplishment. On the contrary, as people such as Ray Charles, Stephen Hawking, and Ron Kovic prove, physical disability can be a spur to greatness rather than a condemnation of emptiness.

In fact, if my experience with physically disabled people can be taken as a guide, as far as accomplishment is concerned, they have a slight edge on the rest of us. The unusual challenges they face require finding greater-than-average sources of energy and determination to achieve much of what able-bodied people take for granted. Often, this ultimately translates into a lifetime of superior performance in whatever endeavor people with disabilities choose to pursue.

If you have watched my Labor Day Telethon over the years, you know exactly what I am talking about. Annually, we introduce to tens of millions of Americans people whose accomplishments would distinguish them regardless of their physical conditions—top-ranking executives, physicians, scientists, lawyers, musicians, and artists. The message I hope the audience receives is not that these extraordinary individuals have achieved what they have by overcoming a dreadful disadvantage that the rest of us are lucky not to have to endure. Rather, I hope our viewers reflect on the fact that these outstanding people have been ennobled and strengthened by the tremendous challenges they have faced.

In 1992, MDA, which has grown over the past four decades into one of the world's leading voluntary health agencies, established a personal achievement awards program to demonstrate to the nation that the distinctive qualities of people with disabilities are by no means confined to the famous. What could have been more appropriate or timely in that year of the implementation of the 1990 Americans with Disabilities Act than to take an action that could perhaps finally achieve the alteration of public perception of disability, which MDA had struggled over four decades to achieve?

On Labor Day, 1992, it was my privilege to introduce to America MDA's inaugural national personal achievement award winner, Steve Mikita, assistant attorney general of the state of Utah. Steve graduated magna cum laude from Duke University as its first wheelchair student in history and was subsequently named the outstanding young lawyer of the year by the Utah Bar Association. After he spoke on the Telethon with an eloquence that caused phones to light up from coast to coast, people asked me where he had been all this time and why they had not known of him before, so deeply impressed were they by him. I answered that he and thousands like him have been here all along. We just have not adequately *noticed* them.

It is my fervent hope that we can eliminate indifference once and for all and make it possible for all of our fellow citizens with disabilities to gain their rightfully high place in our society.

ON FACING CHALLENGES

John Callahan

I was paralyzed for life in 1972, at the age of 21. A friend and I were driving in a Volkswagen on a hot July night, when he smashed the car at full speed into a utility pole. He suffered only minor injuries. But my spinal cord was severed during the crash, leaving me without any feeling from my diaphragm downward. The only muscles I could move were some in my upper body and arms, and I could also extend my fingers. After spending a lot of time in physical therapy, it became possible for me to grasp a pen.

I've always loved to draw. When I was a kid, I made pictures of everything from Daffy Duck (one of my lifelong role models) to caricatures of my teachers and friends. I've always been a people watcher, it seems; and I've always looked at the world in a sort of skewed way. Everything I see just happens to translate immediately into humor. And so, humor has become my way of coping. As the years have gone by, I have developed a tremendous drive to express my humor by drawing cartoons.

The key to cartooning is to put a different spin on the expected, the normal. And that's one reason why many of my cartoons deal with the disabled: amputees, quadriplegics, paraplegics, the blind. The public is not used to seeing them in cartoons.

But there's another reason why my subjects are often disabled men and women. I'm sick and tired of people who presume to speak for the disabled. Call me a cripple, call me a gimp, call me paralyzed for life.

Just don't call me something I'm not. I'm not "differently abled," and my cartoons show that disabled people should not be treated any differently than anyone else.

All of the men, women, and children who are profiled in the Great Achievers series share this in common: their various handicaps have not prevented them from accomplishing great things. Their life stories are worth knowing about because they have found the strength and courage to develop their talents and to follow their dreams as fully as they can.

Whether able-bodied or disabled, a person must strive to overcome obstacles. There's nothing greater than to see a person who faces challenges and conquers them, regardless of his or her limitations.

Around 1920, a Florida laundress washes clothes in large wooden tubs. Ray's mother, Aretha, took in laundry and ironing to support her two children.

1

TWO BROTHERS

THE YEAR WAS 1935. In Greensville, a small country town in northern Florida, two young boys were scurrying through the back woods. Sunlight poured through the trees, the day was hot and humid, but the boys did not seem to mind. Five-year-old Ray Charles Robinson, who was born on September 23, 1930, in Albany, Georgia (and who many years later would drop the "Robinson"), and his four-year-old brother, George, were always together. They were like twins, best friends, barefoot buddies chasing after rabbits, playing hide and seek, throwing pebbles into the lake, and watching spiders spin webs. They lived in a simple one-room shack with their mother, Aretha Robinson, but being poor—dirt poor—did not keep them from feeling happy.

In Greensville (officially named Greenville, but all the townspeople called it Greensville), even on the other side of town where the white folks lived, Mrs. Robinson's boys were known for their special talents.

This photograph from the early 1930s shows the types of goods a small shop in the South often sold. Ray's favorite place to visit in Greensville, the Red Wing Café, had everything from soda water to candy, and he loved to watch Mr. Pit play boogie-woogie on the piano there.

They were gifted children: George was a whiz with numbers, and Ray, whose nickname was Mechanic, loved to climb under cars and trucks to see how the motors worked. Ray had even taught himself how to fix a bicycle, although he did not own one.

Ray found the mechanics of the piano especially fascinating, which was why on this Saturday afternoon the boys stopped by the Red Wing Café, where the owner, Wylie Pitman—Ray called him Mr. Pit—was playing an old upright piano. The café was small. Because it was Saturday, the place was crowded with black men and women who worked during the week at the sawmill, Greensville's major source of employment. Mr. Pit's wife, Miss Georgia, served soda water to the children and beer to the adults; the store had everything from candy to kerosene. There was loud talk over the blaring music, and it was the music that interested Ray as he made his way over to

Mr. Pit, whose fingers danced up and down the keyboard, playing in a lively style called boogie-woogie.

Boogie-woogie made the piano sound like several instruments at once—the pianist's left hand played a bass rhythm pattern while the right hand improvised like crazy. Boogie-woogie was the style that captured Ray's heart as he studied Mr. Pit's fingers flying over the piano.

"Listen, George!" Ray screamed. "Look how that man plays!"

"Come on up here, R. C.," said Mr. Pit—everyone called Ray R. C.—"and try for yourself."

Mr. Pit picked up Ray and put the child on his lap. "You try," he urged. Ray extended his little fingers and started banging—banging hard—with both hands. "No," said Mr. Pit. "You spread out your fingers. Each finger has a separate job to do."

Slowly and patiently, the older man showed Ray how to play a few simple melodies—"Twinkle, Twinkle, Little Star," and "Mary Had a Little Lamb." Still entranced, Ray followed the instructions carefully—he had a good ear and sharp concentration, and he was an eager student.

George stood on the other side of the café, looking a little bored. While his brother fixated on the piano and the adults stood around chatting, George found pieces of discarded wood and wire in the corner of the café. It took him only a few minutes to fashion a miniature wagon, much to the astonishment of Miss Georgia.

"Look what George has done!" she exclaimed, holding up his handiwork.

"He also knows his numbers," added Mr. Pit, as Ray climbed off his lap to look at what his brother had made. "Show how you can add and subtract, George," Mr. Pit urged.

Without the benefit of a day at school, four-year-old George Robinson amazed the folks by adding a long column of numbers and by rattling off his multiplication tables.

"These boys are something, aren't they?" proclaimed Miss Georgia, as she gave them each a piece of candy.

Just as Mr. Pit stopped playing the piano, someone put a few pennies in the jukebox, and suddenly the café was alive again with the sounds of music. Ray raced over to put his ear against the speaker; he would have climbed into the speaker if he could have, because the sounds—more boogie-woogie piano playing by such virtuoso African-American musicians as Pete Johnson, Meade "Lux" Lewis, and Albert Ammons—made him so lighthearted. In addition to recordings of instrumentals, there were those of blues—black country blues by singers called Tampa Red, Blind Boy Phillips, and Washboard Sam. These songs were sometimes happy, sometimes sad—the blues cover a wide range of emotions and are sung with simple expres-

The Bennie Moten Orchestra was popular in the early 1930s. Ray enjoyed listening to the jukebox at the Red Wing Café, which played the records of many outstanding African-American musicians.

sions and strong feelings, close to the emotions of the people gathered together in the Red Wing Café.

Their bellies filled with sweets, Ray and George left the café and headed for home. Puffy rain clouds that looked like cotton candy raced across the summer sky. Somewhere off in the distance, the crackling sound of thunder added excitement to the afternoon. The lush Florida woods—the pecan, chinaberry, and pine trees—smelled fresh and clean. The boys spotted a group of men approaching an especially fat hog, and the flash of a long knife signaled a slaughter. Ray and George stopped for a moment to watch, while squawking chickens scurried by. The big hog was killed quickly; the men shot the animal and then cut its throat. The sight of fresh blood amazed and startled the little boys, who ran, excited and frightened by what they had seen, dashing through the thick woods, losing breath just before they arrived home, and finally stopping in the blackberry patch behind the shack in which they lived with their mother. The berries were in season, ripe, ready to be picked and eaten. Ray and George went at it; they loved the feeling of the fruit in their hands and the taste of juice in their mouths. They grabbed and chewed all they could, their faces smeared, their hearts beating rapidly because they were having so much fun.

"Get out of that patch 'fore a rattlesnake up and bites your head off!" yelled Aretha Robinson as she spotted her boys. She was behind their shack, washing clothes in an enormous tub.

"Rattlesnakes!" the brothers screamed in one voice. They had spotted a few of those long, slithery creatures over the course of the summer, and the idea that one might be underfoot had them racing from the patch into their mother's open arms.

"Now where you children been?" their mother wanted to know.

Breathlessly, Ray and George narrated their adventures to their mother, who, despite her slight frame and sickly

Cotton pickers on a South Carolina plantation labor in a field that surrounds their small dwelling. Aretha Robinson worked in the cotton fields when she was a child; she often told her sons stories from her childhood and about relatives who had been slaves.

nature, was a hardworking woman who took in laundry and ironing to support her small family. Ray talked about the piano lesson from Mr. Pit and the music on the jukebox; George showed his mother the toy wagon he had made and related how he had recited his numbers. Aretha Robinson was proud of her sons.

"I'm making something special tonight," she said. "Something you boys really love. Now go wash up."

Ray and George hurriedly drew water from a small well in the back—there was no indoor plumbing—and cleaned their hands with coarse soap. The air was thick with

humidity, the afternoon breezes had turned into a strong wind; looking west, the boys could see a big storm coming. Inside, though, the aroma of their mother's cooking turned their thoughts to food—the sweet potato pie, the black-eyed peas, the collard greens picked fresh that morning, and the rice smothered in onion gravy.

There was a little argument between the two brothers about who had the bigger portion, but Mrs. Robinson quickly put the bickering to rest by insisting they had each been given exactly the same amount of food. She was a loving but stern parent. When she was a child, she had labored in the tobacco and cotton fields, snapped beans, and hulled peas. Having learned the meaning of hard work, she tolerated little nonsense from her own children. She never married Bailey, the boys' father, a big man who drove steel spikes on the railroad tracks between Florida and Georgia. Bailey did not come to visit the boys often, and, consequently, he was not a part of their daily lives.

The storm hit after dinner. Gusts of hard rain slammed against the shack and water leaked through its thin roof. The boys had heard stories of how tornadoes could uproot trees and hurl whole buildings into the lake. The violence of the storm—flashes of lightning, claps of thunder—scared them, but their mother reassured them. "Don't worry," she said, "This isn't tornado weather."

Aretha Robinson brought both boys into bed with her, holding them tight and telling them stories from her childhood, stories about her own relatives who had been slaves. The brothers were intrigued. After a while, they grew sleepy. The rain had softened and soon the storm passed. Snuggled next to their mother, George fell into a deep, dreamless sleep, while, in his vivid imagination, Ray still heard the red-hot boogie-woogie from Mr. Pit's piano.

When Ray woke up on Sunday morning, he thought of chicken and church. Ray liked them both, and once a week he got both on the same day.

Mrs. Robinson had taught Ray and George to dress themselves, to put on clean shirts and trousers. Shoes were a luxury that she could not afford, however, so the boys wore hand-me-down slippers. The walk to the Shiloh Baptist Church was a short one—less than a half-mile—and the morning was picture perfect. The previous night's rain had gone, the cloudless sky appeared a deep, beautiful blue. Dressed in her good blue dress and wide-brimmed white hat, Mrs. Robinson held her sons' hands as the three of them followed a woodsy path to the church.

Even before they arrived, the music—the singing, the clapping of hands, and the stomping of feet—could be heard through the trees, floating on the cool morning breeze. The rhythmic music, which was overflowing with excitement and enthusiasm, made Ray's heart beat faster. Ray could not wait to get to the small, white wood building that housed the congregation; he skipped ahead of his mother and brother and opened the door to the church so that the sound of singing greeted him full in the face.

The music enchanted Ray—all those voices, men and women, children and old folks, the entire church was a choir, everyone praising God and responding to the call of the preacher. Without musical instruments—there was neither a piano nor an organ in this bare bones country church—the congregation made music of their own, singing gospel hymns and spirituals with so much fire that little

In the South, Baptists, dressed in their Sunday best, gather before a service. Ray loved to go to church, where he was inspired by the singing, clapping of hands, and stomping of feet.

Ray was wild with the rhythm, hardly able to contain himself. The service itself was simple: The minister sermonized and recited from the Bible, and the congregation answered back—calling out encouragement, praising God, waving their hands, breaking into song, and even dancing. The feeling was spontaneous and open. The music was joyful, miraculously allowing people whose lives were far from easy to express a spirit that, at least for the moment, offered relief and nourishment. In 1935, blacks in Greensville, like blacks throughout the Deep South and, for that matter, blacks throughout the United States, endured brutal discrimination on an economic and personal level. Church—especially for little Ray—was both a source of entertainment and inspiration. After the church services, Ray and George, still tingling from the music, ran out the door. As they raced back home, the brothers could almost taste the chicken their mother was about to cook for them.

Meanwhile, Aretha Robinson stopped to chat with one of the church parishioners, a woman who told her about a boy caught stealing food from Mr. Pit's Red Wing Café. The story worried Mrs. Robinson, and when she and her sons arrived home, she told her boys what she had heard. "I know you're good boys," she told them, "but I always want you to remember two things—you do not steal, and you do not beg."

Ray and George saw the seriousness in their mother's eyes and understood what she had said. They also understood that if they did not obey her, she would not hesitate to give them a licking.

"Now go play," she said. "We'll be eating soon. I'm just gonna do a little ironing while the chicken gets done cooking."

The day had turned sticky hot, and the boys, stripped to their shorts, decided to splash around in the tub their mother kept out back for washing clothes. The enormous tub, nearly filled to the top with water, was taller than the boys and could hold only one brother at a time. George climbed over the side and jumped in. As he sank to the bottom of the tub and started making funny little sounds, Ray became distracted by a frog jumping over the grass. He tried to catch the slippery animal but could not; the frog was too quick and unpredictable.

The farther Ray moved from the tub, the more distant became the sounds of George playing in the water. After five minutes or so, Ray looked back toward the tub and realized that something was wrong; his brother seemed to be crying. Running over to George, Ray heard his brother splashing, coughing, and trying to get out of the tub. On tiptoe, Ray peered over the side of the tub to see what had happened: arms flailing the water, legs kicking, George was drowning.

Ray suddenly froze. He did not know what to do, and for a few precious seconds, panic paralyzed him. Finally he reacted and desperately tried to yank his brother out of the tub. But Ray was too small and too weak to grab his brother, so he raced to the house, screaming for his mother. Mrs. Robinson dropped her iron, ran to the tub, and pulled George out. She tried to pump the water out of him; she also tried mouth-to-mouth resuscitation. For a long while she kept trying to revive her son, her forehead covered with sweat and her eyes filled with panic, but George did not respond.

At age four, George had died, and for his best friend and brother, Ray, the world only grew darker. A few months later, Ray Charles Robinson began to go blind.

Some
Views
of the
School

A postcard from the 1930s displays various views of the Florida School for the Deaf and the Blind, located in St. Augustine. Ray became a student at the school in September 1937.

2

THE DARK

IN THE SMALL WAITING ROOM of Dr. McCloud's office, Ray sat next to his mother. It had been more than a year since his brother had died, and Ray's head was filled with troubling thoughts. For months now, after waking up in the morning, his eyes had been covered with thick crust. Aretha Robinson used a damp cloth to wipe Ray's matted eyelids; after about 10 minutes, he would begin blinking and adjusting to the morning light. But there was definitely something wrong with his eyes. Each week he saw less and less. The process was gradual, yet the signs were clear.

There were two doctors in Greensville, both white men, Dr. King and Dr. McCloud. King administered only to white people, whereas McCloud treated blacks as well as whites.

"Will Dr. McCloud be able to help me?" Ray asked his mother.

"I don't know," she replied.

Ray was uneasy during the examination. The doctor appeared before him as a large blob, and Ray could not make out the features on Dr. McCloud's face.

"Tell me what you can and cannot see," the physician told Ray.

"I used to be able to make out people and trees and cars, things like that," Ray explained. "Big things. Then everything got blurred but I could still make out the different colors, the blue in the sky and the green in the grass. Then even the colors got blurred, but I can still see if it's day or night. I know if it's light or dark."

While Ray was speaking, the doctor looked into his eyes with special lights. Ray felt the heat from the instruments; he imagined looking into the burning sun.

When the examination was over, Dr. McCloud prescribed some ointments and eye drops, hoping that these medications would be of some help. Weeks passed, however, and nothing seemed to aid Ray's condition. Eventually, Dr. McCloud recommended that Mrs. Robinson take her son to a clinic in Madison, not far from Greensville. Mother and son went to the doctor's office in Madison, where Ray was thoroughly examined. Mrs. Robinson turned to the doctor and said, "Tell me, is there hope?"

The doctor paused a long while before he replied. "I'm afraid not, Mrs. Robinson. Your boy is losing his sight."

"But what about cures?" asked Aretha Robinson. "There must be cures."

"I don't know of any," answered the physician, who believed that the blindness was being caused by a disease known as glaucoma.

"I understand," she replied.

Aretha Robinson took Ray by the hand and led him out of the clinic. When they reached Greensville, they walked down the main street of town—past the bank, the post office, the general store, and across the railroad tracks, back into the woods and into their one-room shack. Aretha

Robinson had said nothing to her son until they were in the privacy of their home.

"This is not the end of the world," she told Ray. "I'm not saying it's going to be easy, but it's not going to be impossible. You aren't dying. You're losing your sight, not your mind. The rest of your body works fine. Your mind is good, Ray. You can still do whatever you want to do. But I'm going to have to teach you, and you're going to have to pay special attention. I'm going to teach you to cook and clean and do all your chores like any other child. And the reason I'm going to teach you is 'cause I won't always be around to do for you."

"Don't say that," Ray protested. "You'll always be here."

"No, I won't. You got to know that. And when I'm gone, you're gonna have to do for yourself. Understand?"

Mrs. Robinson reached down and hugged her son with all the strength of her frail body. She kissed his forehead and said, "I love you and I'm going to help you. I'm going to help you do for yourself."

A week later, on a Saturday morning, a woman named Mary Jane came to visit. Mary Jane was Aretha Robinson's age and once had been married to Bailey, Ray's father. Over the years she had grown especially fond of Ray. In fact, the two were so close that, although he called Aretha "Mama," he referred to Mary Jane as "Mother."

Ray responded to Mary Jane's knock on the door. He had a scrub brush in his hand when she entered the shack and she saw how his eyes were squeezed together, closed tight. "What in the world are you doing?" she asked.

"Scrubbing the floor, like Mama showed me," answered Ray.

"Your mama shouldn't be making you do stuff like that," said Mary Jane, handing Ray several pieces of his favorite chocolate.

"Why not?" asked Mrs. Robinson, who had just arrived from town. The two women were friendly but differed greatly when it came to raising Ray. Aretha Robinson was a strict disciplinarian, whereas Mary Jane was extremely lenient. In different ways and for different reasons, Ray loved both women.

"Everyone's talkin' 'bout how you are treating this boy like he can see," said Mary Jane.

"Not seeing don't keep him from playing the piano, does it?" Aretha asked.

"I love playing the piano," Ray interjected.

"But he shouldn't be . . . " Mary Jane started to argue.

"He should be doing what most other kids are doing because he's as smart and strong as any of them," Aretha tersely replied.

"Look 'Retha," Mary Jane tried to explain, "I know about strong. I'm working over at the sawmill right beside all those men, doing the same heavy hauling as them. But being blind is different."

"It's different," countered Aretha, "only in that the blind gotta go to different schools. That's what I been talkin' to the folks in town about. They say there's a school in St. Augustine, a state school for the deaf and the blind. They say that's where Ray should be going to school. That's where he gotta get his education."

"But St. Augustine is far away," said Ray.

"You'll go there to live," explained his mother. "All the kids live at school."

"But I wanna stay here . . ."

"It ain't right, 'Retha, to be sending a blind boy away from home," Mary Jane protested.

"What ain't right," Aretha replied, "is keeping Ray away from learning."

The days that followed were not easy for Ray. He knew there was no changing his mother's mind. He spent a lot of time with Mary Jane, who comforted him by cooking his favorite meals. At Mary Jane's house, there were no errands to run, no cleaning up to do, and no pressures. He wished he could live there or continue to live with his

Blind students play on the grounds of the St. Augustine school. Aretha Robinson wanted Ray to get an education, and she realized he needed special teachers like those in St. Augustine who knew how to instruct blind students to read and write.

mother. It seemed as though anything would be better than having to go away to school.

Ray shuddered every time he thought about attending the Florida School for the Deaf and the Blind. He understood that he could not continue to go to a regular school; the teachers there did not know how to teach a blind person to read or write. But what about his friends? He did not want to leave them. And what about Mr. Pit, the man who always let him play the piano? What would he do without Mr. Pit and the Red Wing Café? Who else could show him music, the kind of boogie-woogie music Ray loved so much? Ray imagined that going away to school was worse than going blind.

Finally, in the fall of 1937, the day came. Ray's pleas did him no good. Aretha Robinson had done all she could to make him independent. This was the most difficult step for them both. Mrs. Robinson did not want to relinquish hold of her son, and yet she knew—to be responsible, to secure his survival—she had no choice but to let him go. She realized that Ray needed a decent education more than he needed her daily companionship. So far, he had responded well to the way in which she had pushed him out into the world. Ray was able to walk alone to his friends' homes; he traveled into town himself, taking little steps, cautiously making his way over a landscape that he had learned by feel—a tree here, a row of bushes there. Aretha Robinson had even seen her son ride a bicycle by himself.

The neighbors were amazed by, and some were even scornful of, Mrs. Robinson's attitude, but their opinions were beside the point. She was pleased that her son had displayed the confidence to ride the bicycle in an open field, his buddies giving him verbal instructions on how and where to direct the two-wheeler. Ray continued to show talent at the piano, and his interest in mechanics— taking apart engines of any kind—was keen. He lacked only sight.

By the fall of 1937, he was almost completely blind, able only to see bright lights. Mrs. Robinson knew he needed special instruction and there was no going back. The train was leaving for St. Augustine, located 160 miles east of Greensville, and Ray, only seven years old, was leaving home for the first time in his life.

*   *   *

It was a drizzly September morning. Aretha Robinson, Mary Jane, and Ray waited at the Greensville train station. Ray held a small knapsack containing all of his possessions. His stomach was in knots. His eyes were almost completely shut and he could only see the murky gray of day. He reached out and first felt his mother's face, then Mary Jane's hand. Both women bent down and hugged him, kissed him, and assured him that everything was going to be all right. Ray, however, was not so sure. He had never been on a train before, never left Greensville, and never known what it meant to travel. In the distance he heard the mournful whistle of the approaching train, the cars rumbling closer and closer until Ray felt the wind from the powerful locomotive pulling into the station. He could make out only a streak of blurred colors. Tears ran down his cheeks, and his mother and Mary Jane were also crying.

"Don't be afraid," said Aretha Robinson. "This is a special train with a special compartment."

As Aretha and Mary Jane followed, a porter led Ray to the section of the train reserved for other children going to the Florida School for the Deaf and the Blind in St. Augustine.

"I love you," said his mother, who kissed Ray for the last time.

"I love you, monkey doodle," said Mary Jane, as she embraced Ray.

Ray cried so hard he could not talk. The porter picked him up, carried him into the train, and set him beside another little blind boy. For the next four hours, Ray did not open his mouth, his heart was still heavy, his stomach was nervous, his cheeks soaked with tears.

Adjusting to a new school, a new city, and a new environment would not be easy. Ray was thrown in with strangers, people he could not see. To make matters more baffling, there were several layers of segregation at the school. First, all the blacks were separated from the whites, then the blind were isolated from the deaf, and finally the girls were segregated from the boys.

In the black group there were 35 children, who, for the next eight years, would be Ray's constant companions, his new family. They lived in a dormitory. Everyone was friendly enough, everyone seemed to know each other, but because Ray was new to the school he felt frightened and homesick each hour of every day.

Ray spent the first couple of weeks crying and sulking. No one could console him, and he did not want to meet any of the kids at school. He could not stop thinking of his mother, Mary Jane, and his friends back in Greenville. He also thought about church and playing Mr. Pit's piano. Some of the kids were cruel, and his new companions, instead of calling him R. C., referred to him as "sissy boy" or "Mama's baby." Ray tried to pay no attention to them and to stay to himself, but the school routine was demanding and before long, little by little, he began adjusting to his new surroundings.

"One thing about me," Ray said years later about his early life, "I do adapt. Sure it was a struggle, but I somehow muddled through the emotional mess. I finally realized I had no choice."

At the state school for the blind, the day started at 5:30 A.M., and the routine was rigid. Ray responded well to the discipline, quickly learning braille, a system of writing made up of raised dots that enables the blind to read and write. After only 10 days of instruction, Ray read his first books, called primers: *Living on John's Farm* and *The White Rabbit*. For the rest of his life, Ray would be an avid reader. He also proved adept at workshop—carving wood, weaving cane for the seats of chairs, and putting together brooms, mops, pot holders, and leather purses. There was exercise in the afternoons, races, and even a special type

The Florida School for the Deaf and the Blind was segregated: the deaf were separated from the blind, whites from the blacks, and boys from the girls. This photograph shows one of the vocational training classes. Ray enjoyed workshop, where he learned to carve wood, make brooms, and weave cane for the seats of chairs.

of football. Ray began to make friends with a boy named Clarence and another named Joe, who was his bunk mate. For Ray, the best part of school, however, was the music area—a room with a piano, a few other instruments, and the teachers who immediately recognized his talent. Music and math proved to be Ray's best subjects.

The first few months at school went by quickly. Although Ray realized that even among other poor children he was the poorest—he had so few clothes that he had to accept hand-me-downs from the state—he still managed to cope with the situation; that is, until the holidays arrived. A week before Christmas, all the students returned home to be with their families for two weeks. Everyone except Ray. Although the state of Florida paid for transportation to and from school in September and June, the students had to pay their own way if they wished to go home for Christmas. Mrs. Robinson did not have the money to send for her son, and consequently, Ray spent the last weeks of 1937 alone, with nothing to do and no one to talk to. Only a skeleton crew remained at the school. Days seemed to drag on forever, and Ray found himself sobbing, just as he had during his first days at school. He imagined everyone at home, families gathered around tables, the lights of Christmas trees, and the exchange of gifts. Never had he felt more isolated, more dejected. At long last, when his schoolmates returned in early January he was elated, warmly embracing the same kids he had been so reluctant to become acquainted with in September.

The next semester, however, brought a new sort of pain: Ray's right eye began to ache. The throbbing became more and more intense until the school doctor decided that the diseased eye had to be removed. Even though Ray could not see out of the eye, the thought of removing it altogether was horrifying, even more frightening than the idea of going blind, which, after all, had been a gradual process. Nonetheless, Ray had no choice. The pain became overwhelming and the eye had to be extracted. Ray's operation

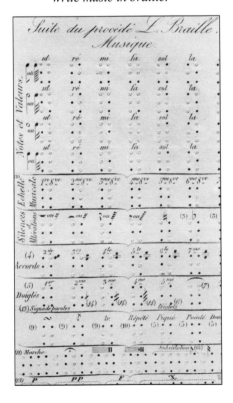

This musical composition has notations written in braille, a system using a raised-dot alphabet that was invented by Louis Braille of France in the 1820s. At school, Ray learned to read and write music in braille.

was successful, and after a week or so of recovery, he was back at his daily routine. He had suffered through yet another ordeal and had been able to make another major adjustment.

When summer vacation arrived, Ray anxiously made the journey back to Greensville. At the end of the long train ride, Aretha Robinson, Mary Jane, and Ray's friends were waiting with open arms. Even though he was now totally blind, Ray sensed the colors of the Greensville landscape he knew so well, the smells, and the feeling of the dirt roads under his bare feet. With perfect accuracy, he recalled the location of everything—the Shiloh Baptist Church, the Red Wing Café, the creeks and ponds, and the secret hiding place in the back woods. He ran off to play like any other child, as though his vision were perfect. He was back in his old routine in no time, often spending the night with Mary Jane, who plied him with bologna, hot dogs, and candies—treats that his mother could not afford. At home, under his mother's loving but stern care, Ray's former chores awaited him.

One of Ray's jobs was to scrub and mop the floor. Years later Ray recalled an incident concerning this task. One morning, anxious to meet up with his pals, Ray decided to take a short cut in doing the mopping: he threw water on the floor, sloshed it around, and then mopped, avoiding the hardest part of the job, the scrubbing. He spent the rest of the day bicycle riding. That night when Ray returned home, his mother was waiting for him and she was furious. "If I ask you to do a job," she told her son, "I expect it done right. Now start from scratch, and this time *scrub!*"

Ray began to realize that it was his mother—and only his mother—who could control the wild side of his nature; it was she who taught him discipline and made him understand rules. As a result, he was able to do well at school.

In the fall of 1938, Ray started his second year at the Florida School for the Deaf and the Blind, and his attitude

Artie Shaw, seen here in the 1941 movie Second Chorus, *so impressed 10-year-old Ray with his masterful playing of the clarinet that Ray took up the instrument himself.*

had vastly improved. He was happy, even eager, to return to St. Augustine. He discovered he was popular among the other students, who nicknamed him Foots because he ran around in his bare feet. Music continued to be Ray's favorite subject and, although only eight years old, he set exceedingly high standards for himself. Using braille, he learned to read and write music, although the boogie-woogie and blues styles he loved so well were prohibited at school. His teachers taught him classical compositions, including simple melodies by Frédéric Chopin and waltzes by Johann Strauss. He loved classical music—actually, every kind of music fascinated Ray. On the radio in the boys' dorm, he heard the big-band jazz that was so popular in the United States during the 1930s, played by white big bands that were modeled on—and often copied—black bands, such as Jimmie Lunceford, Count Basie, Lucky Millinder, and Duke Ellington. Among these white bands were those of trombonists Glenn Miller and Tommy Dorsey and the clarinetists Benny Goodman and Artie Shaw. Shaw made a special impression on young Ray, who, at age 10, took up the clarinet himself, just because he loved Artie's playing so deeply, especially his rendi-

In the 1930s, music performed by black bands like Count Basie's (Basie is seated at piano) was often copied by white bands, and Ray loved to listen to recordings on the radio in the boys' dormitory.

tions of "Stardust" and "Concerto for Clarinet." Later Ray also learned to play the alto saxophone.

Aside from his regular music teachers at school, Ray also learned piano from some of the students, or the "big boys" as Ray called them. The most proficient of these was Joe Lee Lawrence, a teenager who played in the extravagant style of Art Tatum, whom most people consider to be the greatest virtuoso in the history of jazz piano. Over the years, Ray, like many young pianists, would refer to Tatum as "God." The other great stylist of the period was Thomas "Fats" Waller, whose bawdy, sophisticated humor and happy swing music made him a major model for countless other jazz and blues keyboardists. Waller was also a songwriter—he wrote American classics like "Ain't Misbehavin'" and "Honeysuckle Rose"—and Ray felt his positive influence early on.

"I never thought about being famous," Charles later claimed, "but I always wanted to be great. My thing was musicianship. I was impressed by anyone who mastered his instrument. I wanted the respect of the other musicians. I wanted to be known as someone who could really play."

As early as age 9 or 10, Ray started to become interested in girls. He liked to flirt with them and tease them, and he was always trying to convince them to sneak into the music practice room with him. Ray took his first loves seriously. At a young age he was touched by romance. He was not only physically attracted to girls, but emotionally attracted as well, and their company comforted him.

Other blind boys used what Ray called the braille method in getting next to girls, using their hands to feel the girls' faces and bodies after being introduced. Ray found this crude and overbearing. Instead, he claimed that by merely touching a girl's hand above her wrist he could tell the proportion of the rest of her body.

"Engines and women," Charles said as an adult, "were two things I've never grown tired of exploring—not as a child, not now, not ever."

Ray's teachers thought he was a bit mischievous; and he was certainly curious and adventuresome. At age 10, he began wandering off-campus by himself without the aid of a cane or a guide dog. Ray never wanted to appear helpless—his mother had taught him that. He never learned to play guitar because some blind singers, such as Blind Lemon Jefferson, were noted for playing the guitar and Ray did not want that stigma placed upon him. Ray just wanted to be Ray. He wanted to explore.

The first time he went into St. Augustine, he was accompanied by a sighted person. He made mental notes about the location of certain buildings, streets, and stairs. In his mind he compared it to memorizing a musical score in braille: first one learns five bars, then another five,

Art Tatum performs at a club. Many young pianists, such as Ray, admired, even idolized, Tatum because of his proficiency on the piano, referring to him as "God."

A women's club in Florida puts on an outdoor activity. Ray's first job was playing the piano and singing for ladies' tea parties in St. Augustine.

then perhaps ten bars, until the full composition is in one's head. In no time he had the map of the city etched in his mind and could go off on his own, displaying his peculiar combination of caution and nerve—caution when he came to a street corner, listening carefully until all the cars had passed; nerve when it came to seeking work off-campus.

Charles's first job was playing for black ladies' tea parties. The women were charmed by his talent and his ability to play popular hits of the day, such as "String of Pearls" and "Jersey Bounce," and they gave him candies and tangerines (his favorite fruit) as well as small change. He was thrilled to earn a dollar in a single afternoon.

Even as a child, Ray's musical tastes were broad. He had no prejudices when it came to sounds. On Saturday nights, he always listened to the "Grand Ole Opry," a program of white country music known as hillbilly, that was broadcast on radio. Artists such as Hank Williams, Hank Snow, Jimmie Rodgers, and Roy Acuff touched Ray's soul. White pop singers, including Bing Crosby, Dick Haymes, Vaughn Monroe, and Tony Martin, might have been considered corny by some, but Ray appreciated the smoothness of their styles. Naturally he loved black church music, which he had been hearing and singing his whole life, and harmonizing groups like Wings over Jordan and the Golden Gate Quartet. And, of course, the geniuses of the black big-band orchestras—Count Basie, Duke Ellington, Jimmie Lunceford, Jay McShann, Lucky Millinder, and Chick Webb—helped shape Ray's musical mind. As Ray entered his teen years, his music—both the classical pieces he learned at school and the pop/jazz he played off-campus—became more sophisticated.

Besides Mr. Pit and Miss Georgia, another couple from home were especially fond of Ray. Henry Johnson and his wife, Alice, moved to Tallahassee, 40 miles west of Greensville, and often invited Ray to spend part of the summer with them. They owned a club with a jukebox, from which Ray found himself memorizing every song. Mr. Johnson was a member of a fraternal organization, and it raised money to buy Ray a new clarinet. Ray was ecstatic. Another family—Mr. Bison, his wife, Dolly, and his daughter, Lucille—owned a grocery store, and they, too, befriended Ray. They taught him to use their cash register and actually had him ringing up sales and giving change to customers. Through other friends in Tallahassee, Ray learned to drive a motorcycle and a car. With someone seated next to him, describing the terrain, he was able to operate the vehicles as well as a sighted person. If he knew the territory extremely well, he would even drive by himself.

Learning to trust himself was one of the great lessons of Ray's childhood. Once in St. Augustine, for example, he and a friend were about to cross a street. Ray thought

Duke Ellington (at the piano) and his band were at the forefront of jazz. Many of Ellington's works, such as "Mood Indigo" and "Sophisticated Lady," became classics, and their style greatly influenced young Ray.

he had heard some noise; his friend, however, who had partial sight, assured him no traffic was coming. But as they stepped off the curb, an approaching car struck Ray and threw him several feet into the air. Miraculously, he was not hurt. But he learned his lesson: in the future, he would trust his own ears.

During this period, Ray was increasingly drawn to two singer-pianists, artists who would greatly influence his early musical style. The first was Charles Brown, an extremely gifted musician whose vocals with Johnny Moore and the Three Blazes—especially a number called "Drifting Blues"—had a lasting impact on Ray. Ray would sing the song throughout his career and, as a child, he did a letter-perfect imitation of Brown's slow, drawling, behind-the-beat vocals.

Ray Charles's greatest idol, however, was Nat "King" Cole. For young Ray, Cole had everything: He was a brilliant pianist—a brilliant *jazz* pianist—who could play in virtually every style, from boogie-woogie to swing to the emerging modern sound of the 1940s known as bebop. Cole's velvet-smooth voice was sweet, seductive, and, although true to jazz phrasing, extended beyond jazz to the lucrative field of popular music. Although Nat Cole's music had a huge following in the black community, it also found a large audience outside of it, a fact not lost on young Ray. He understood that white people usually had the cash to buy the records, and that a black artist had a far better chance of making money if his style pleased everyone. Nat Cole accomplished this—his records sold across the board—and, furthermore, he had the respect of his fellow musicians.

Cole's first success came with a trio—piano, bass, and guitar (no drums, which, with piano and bass, make up the traditional rhythm section in a band)—a configuration that fascinated Ray. In fact, as a teenager Ray learned the King Cole repertoire, tunes such as "Straighten Up and Fly Right" and "Sweet Lorraine," memorizing and imitating the most subtle nuances of Cole's extremely sophisticated vocal phrasing and piano playing. "No one accompanied himself like Nat Cole," Charles later observed. "He was the one who taught me how to fill in piano around my voice." In the small social clubs and parties where Ray entertained off campus and during vacations, the highlight was invariably his rendition of the master's latest hit.

Charles Brown was a gifted singer whom Ray emulated, especially his rendition of "Drifting Blues." Ray was able to imitate Brown's slow, drawling, behind-the-beat vocals.

The King Cole Trio affected Ray the most, as far as his repertoire was concerned. Nat "King" Cole (right), who led the trio, was a brilliant pianist and could play in almost every style. His velvet-smooth voice extended beyond jazz to the field of popular music.

"My Lord," the ladies would say, "that child sounds *exactly* like King Cole!"

Ray appreciated the comments. After all, imitating Nat Cole was Ray's main ambition. With each passing year, he felt more confident, learned his lessons at school, became a quick reader and a good writer, made friends with his fellow students, and pursued his two greatest passions—girls and music—with happy determination. He enjoyed playing dominoes and had even invented his own method of brailleing playing cards. Things were going well for Ray—until the middle of May 1945.

Ray, who was 14 years old at the time, was sitting in class when his teacher asked some questions about a novel, *The Adventures of Huckleberry Finn,* that the students had just read. Ray liked the Mark Twain story, which was about a white boy and a black runaway slave. Ray's mind was on the story, when a monitor came to the classroom to say that Ray was wanted in the principal's office. Ray's first thought was that he had done something wrong and was going to be reprimanded. His stomach became queasy as he walked across campus.

The principal had a deep voice and a slow way of talking.

"Ray Charles Robinson," he said somberly.

"Yes, sir," Ray replied.

"I'm afraid I have bad news."

Ray said nothing and waited for what the principal would say next.

"Your mother," he began, taking a deep breath before going on, "your mother . . . your mother is dead."

Ray felt as though he had been hit in the face with a brick. His throat went dry, his heart started to race; shock, fear, and pain shot through his body. "My mother can't be dead," he finally said.

"She died last night," the principal explained.

"But she wasn't sick, no one said she was sick, she can't be, she just can't be."

The principal came out from behind his desk and put his arm around Ray. "I'm sorry," he said. "Very sorry."

Ray's head spun. He felt dizzy, nauseous, terrified, and lost. He barely heard the principal say, "We'll arrange for you to go home for the funeral."

Ray was sure he had dreamed the entire conversation. In a second or two he would wake up and snap out of it. In a few weeks, school would be over and he would go home to see his mother. In a few weeks, he and his mother would be together again. Everything was going to be all right. It had to be. His mother could not be dead—she would not leave without first saying good-bye. She would not do that, not *his* mother.

Jacksonville, Florida's most populous city, is seen here in a rainy night scene, neon signs ablaze, in 1946. After the death of his mother in 1945, Ray decided to start his music career in Jacksonville.

3

STARTING OUT

RAY WAS DISORIENTED on the long train ride home and was lost in his thoughts when he arrived in Greensville. Nothing seemed real or right to him. He walked around in a trance. Mary Jane came to the train station. She tried to comfort him, but there was no comforting. There was nothing to say. A lump had formed in the middle of Ray's throat that prevented him from talking. He had no desire to speak; he had no appetite. He could not accept the fact that he could not tell his mother good-bye. The last time he had seen her was at Christmas, more than five months earlier. Her death seemed too sudden, cruel, and unfair. He went to her funeral, which was attended by whites as well as blacks, and stood like a zombie at the memorial service. Words did not leave his mouth and tears did not flow. He reached out and touched his mother's face one last time while chills ran over his body.

Days passed. Ray did not talk, he barely ate, and he sat by himself, remembering his mother's appearance, her voice, the texture of her hair, the smell of her skin, and the way she had kissed him good-night every day of his life until he had gone off to school. He knew she had been frail and sick. She was only 32, certainly too young to die. In his dreams, she magically reappeared and walked the earth like a natural woman. When he awoke, though, he tried to face the truth, but he could not. He did not believe he could go on.

Neighbors and friends, such as Mr. Pit and Miss Georgia, were worried about Ray and they tried to comfort him. Dr. McCloud explained to him that his mother had died of a heart attack. Ray listened to the doctor's words, but he still could not accept their meaning. His moping and mourning grew so deep that he was barely able to function. Alarmed by his behavior, everyone realized that he was getting sick and people feared he was becoming dangerous to himself. Then Ma Beck came to speak with Ray.

Ma Beck had had 22 children, three of whom had died and 9 sons and 10 daughters who were still living. The townspeople believed that Ma Beck was the most spiritual person in Greensville; everyone loved and respected her. She was the salt of the earth. When she spoke, folks listened, and when she talked to Ray, her words were strong and firm.

"Look here, boy," she said, "Don't you remember what your mama told you? Well, you better. Your mama wouldn't want you acting this way. You know the things she taught you. You been acting like a crazy boy, and if she was here, she wouldn't put up with it. Stop acting like a crazy boy. Stop feeling sorry for yourself. Your mama spent her whole life preparing you for this day. You know what she taught you. She taught you to carry on. Alone. And that's all there is to it. You gotta carry on, R. C."

Ma Beck's lecture finally broke Ray, and tears streamed from his eyes; he cried and sobbed and shook for a long,

long time as Ma Beck held him to her bosom and softly rocked him back and forth. "Yes, child, yes, yes, it'll be all right," she said; "believe me it's gonna be all right."

It took a while, but Ray's good sense returned. The void left by his mother's death would never go away; the pain, like the loss of his brother, would remain with him forever, yet little by little he began thinking clearly, remembering certain words she had said. "You will not beg and you will not steal," he recalled her saying. "You gotta believe that you can do what you can do."

The summer months after his mother's death were a critical time in Ray's life. He remained in Greensville and wandered about, trying to decide what to do next. His good friends were a comfort and tried to keep him busy; however, when they offered sympathy, Ray rebuffed them. He did not want anyone to feel sorry for him. Mary Jane asked him to stay in Greensville and live with her, but Ray was hesitant. Even though he loved her like a mother, Mary Jane was not, after all, his real mother. And as far as Greensville was concerned, it was his home, and home was reassuring, but it now seemed small to him. After having gone to school in St. Augustine and having spent summers in Tallahassee, Ray had encountered more of the world. He liked those experiences. Furthermore, he had learned that people appreciated his music.

As the fall of 1945 approached, Ray carefully contemplated his next move. He had not graduated from school, and going back to St. Augustine would be the easiest path to follow. He had been a student at the state school for eight years and knew every inch of the campus. He was a popular student, and, financially, the school did not cost him anything. The school was a refuge.

On the other hand, Ray had become a little bored with school. Although he received decent grades, his studies did not excite him. If his mother were alive, he would not dream of quitting—she would never have permitted it. Left on his own, however, Ray was faced with his first major dilemma: he had to decide what course his life would take. The quandary both worried and excited him. Late in August, Ray left Greensville for Tallahassee, where he did some heavy thinking.

When he returned to Greensville, Ray had made up his mind. He decided not to return to school but was determined to go out into the world to earn money making music. He knew he was a good musician and he believed that the time had come to find out just how good.

"How are you going to get around without help?" asked a neighbor.

"We'll chip in and buy you a Seeing Eye dog," said another.

Ray, however, refused the offer. No dog, no cane.

By chance, Mary Jane had friends, the Thompsons, in Jacksonville, the most populous city in Florida. The Thompsons had agreed to let Ray stay with them, so he decided to start his career there.

He packed the clarinet Mr. Johnson's lodge brothers had bought for him, two shirts, two pairs of pants, underwear, socks, and his old pair of sneakers. Mary Jane walked him to the station. He was apprehensive and scared, but he began to feel something new, an emotion that made him feel like the music he loved so passionately, a spirit that could not easily be explained. Ray felt the spirit of the music burning inside him, a spirit that drove him on. For the first time in his life, he had faith in himself.

When he arrived in Jacksonville, Ray found his way to the Musicians' Local Union Hall #632, which was located near downtown. This was a black union—segregation was still in practice in 1945—where musicians could spend some leisure time, trade gossip, play checkers, or practice their instruments. An upright piano stood in the corner of the hall and several of the old-timers noticed that a young blind man had been sitting at the piano nearly every day. He played songs in all styles, including blues, boogie-woogie, and swing, and, even though he was young, his fingers ran over the keys like a professional's. On this particular day, Henry Washington, a drummer, heard the young Ray Charles toying with "One O'Clock Jump," one of Count Basie's songs.

"Sounds pretty good," said Washington.

"Thank you, sir," said Ray.

"You live around here?" asked Washington.

"I come from Greensville, but now I'm living in Jacksonville," Ray explained, "living with Mr. and Mrs. Thompson over on West Church Street. Not far from here."

"Let me ask you something," said Washington. "How does a blind boy make his way around a big city like this?"

"Well, sir, Mr. Thompson was good enough to take me over here a couple of times, and when he did, I paid real good attention to the drainage pipes and sewers and cracks in the pavement. They're my markers. Now I can walk over here by myself whenever I want."

"And play this here piano for free, hoping someone will notice you. Is that it?" Washington asked.

"I'm glad *you* noticed. 'Cause I'm looking for work." Ray replied.

"I figured as much. That's why I'm talkin' to you. See, I got a band . . ."

"And you need a piano player?" Ray asked eagerly.

"Part-time, son, it's only part-time."

Ray did not care whether it was part-time or not; he was ecstatic about getting work. At home that evening, over dinner, he told the Thompsons and Louise—who was Mrs. Thompson's sister and Mary Jane's best friend, and whom Ray called Big Sister—all about Henry Washington and his big band. Everyone was excited about Ray's news and congratulated him.

Later in the evening, listening to his favorite radio programs, a suspense drama called "The Shadow" and the comedy "Amos 'n' Andy," Ray could think only about playing music with a real band.

It turned out, however, that the job was at the Two Spot, a club that served liquor, and anyone who was under the age of 21 was not allowed in. Washington fudged the rules and let Ray sit in with the band, whose syncopated swing resembled Count Basie's. Washington even allowed Ray to play his Nat Cole/Charles Brown–style songs. The audience appreciated Ray's music, but the club owner, who was worried about the law, kept Ray from returning to the club.

Shortly thereafter, Ray met Tiny York, an entertainer who modeled himself after Louis Jordan. Jordan was tremendously popular among African Americans during the 1940s as an alto saxophonist, combo leader, singer, and composer of witty songs. Jordan had formulated a new sort of music, steeped in swing rhythms but rich in references to the realities and joys of everyday black life. His big hits—"Saturday Night Fish Fry," "Ain't Nobody Here But Us Chickens," and "Let the Good Times Roll"—led to an emerging category of music that would become known later in the 1940s as rhythm and blues and that, in turn, would give birth in the 1950s to the worldwide phenomenon known as rock and roll. Tiny York, like so many other musicians at the time—including Ray Charles—had been captivated by Louis Jordan and his sound. Glad to have his first halfway-steady job, Ray joined Union #632, becoming a professional, and began his work with Tiny York.

Almost everyone around Ray was older than he by at least 5 to 10 years. Ray, excited about being able to play in clubs till midnight or later, started to feel more mature, and quickly learned to take responsibility for himself. When Ray received his pay, for example, he asked for payment in one-dollar bills, enabling him to carefully count out the money himself. He became more self-reliant and his confidence grew. It was the joy of the songs, however, the exhilaration of swing, the musical expression of his feelings—the satisfaction of having an outlet for his many emotions—that kept him focused on finding work.

Tiny York and his band, with Ray Charles on piano, hit the road and found their way to Orlando, a major city in central Florida. Ray soon learned one of the liabilities of life on the road: when they reached Orlando, they discovered that their engagements had been canceled and the band members were left stranded. Some of the musicians had enough money to return to Jacksonville; others did not. Ray decided to remain in Orlando because, although he enjoyed living with the Thompsons, who had treated him like he was their own son, he worried about growing too dependent on them. The older Ray became, the more he

Customers at a popular nightclub kick up their heels while a bandleader shakes maracas to the swinging beat of the music. Ray's first job in Jacksonville was at the Two Spot, a club that served liquor; however, because he was underage, the club owner only allowed him to appear onstage once

Louis Jordan, a bandleader, singer, composer, and alto saxophonist, was extremely popular during the 1940s. Many musicians, including Ray, were influenced by his swing rhythms in such hits as "Saturday Night Fish Fry" and "Let the Good Times Roll."

clung to the idea of remaining independent—even if that meant he would have to endure suffering.

At 16, Ray struggled in Orlando. He rented a room for three dollars a week, and because there was not much work, he had little money to buy food. He could often only afford to purchase a few soda crackers and a can of sardines. Sometimes, chipping in with other musicians, he bought a six-cent bag of beans, cooked them up with fatback, salt, and pepper, and considered the dish a banquet.

Alone, he frequently explored the streets of Orlando, using the same methods he had employed in Tallahassee and Jacksonville. If he wanted to cross a busy street, he waited until a group of people came along—preferably women—inserted himself in the middle of the group, and walked with them. He relied on his other senses—hearing, smell, and touch—to guide him. Hunger lingered, meanwhile, but the thought of selling pencils on the street corner repulsed him. Ray did not want to be pitied. He was a good musician and sooner or later work would come.

It took Ray longer than he expected to find a job. Times were especially tough because the men who had left their jobs to fight in the American armed forces during World War II began returning home now that the war was ending. The Orlando area became flooded with good musicians. But after scuffling around town and hanging out in the nightclubs where he always asked for work, Ray finally met Joe Anderson, whose big band played at the Sunshine Club. Anderson invited Ray to join them at the club— Ray's only stroke of luck in the city.

Anderson's band was modeled after the orchestra of clarinetist Woody Herman. It was a modern, first-rate group, but most of the musical arrangements were stock, meaning that they could be purchased in any music store. When Anderson discovered that Ray could write music, a skill he had learned in school, he asked Ray to compose original arrangements for the band. Ray leaped at the chance to use his talent.

Ray's musical intelligence was so keen that he had the capacity to write a musical arrangement entirely in his head. With a fellow musician acting as his secretary, he called off every note to be played by every instrumentalist in the band—in all, 16 different parts. In his mind, Ray heard how one part blended with all the others. He worked diligently, reasoning that by adding the qualification of arranger to his résumé with those of pianist and singer, his chances of finding future work would improve.

Ray found additional work with a couple of combos, groups led by Sammy Glover and A. C. Price, in Atlanta, Georgia. Some of the places where the combos played were dangerous. People drank hard, fights broke out, and even shootings occurred. Ray learned to locate the exits as soon as he entered the clubs, and if the disturbances became violent, he would head for the escape routes without haste. He was even known to jump out windows.

Most of the excitement at the clubs, though, was in the music. In addition to the paid gigs (the word musicians use for "jobs"), Ray looked for jam sessions. At a jam session, musicians get together and improvise, for their own stimulation and for the sheer joy of expressing and sharing musical ideas. In the late 1940s, competition among musicians was fierce. Two historical and stylistic periods of jazz met head on—swing and the newer style, bebop—with musicianship reaching an all-time high. (Bebop was the radically modern jazz invented by experimenters such as Dizzy Gillespie and Charlie Parker.) Ray thrived in such an environment. On the bandstand, playing piano behind a tenor saxophonist, trombonist, guitarist, bassist, and drummer, Ray improvised with the best of them. Ad-libbing, inventing on the spot, he loved the element of surprise, not knowing what song would be played next, switching from key to key, keeping up with the mood of the moment. Bebop motifs like "Lady Be Good," "Body and Soul," and "How High the Moon" were played at ferociously fast tempos. The melodies were based upon

An Orlando, Florida, band-leader Lucky Millinder (right), whom many considered to be in the top rank of musicians, allowed Ray to audition for his band. After the young man's performance, Millinder told a stunned Ray, "You ain't good enough . . . you don't got what it takes."

complex and challenging chord changes, and the technical demands on the musicians were enormous. The air was charged with drama and the music crackled with emotional fire.

Even though Ray struggled financially at this time, his self-esteem rose. He was already considered to be an excellent musician by his peers, so when he heard that Lucky Millinder, the leader of a nationally acclaimed big band, was coming through Orlando, he decided to meet the man and audition for him.

Ray had been listening to Millinder's band for years. He knew Millinder's material and especially liked "That's All," a big hit in 1941 recorded by Lucky and his vocalist

Rosetta Tharpe. Millinder and his band were in the top rank of musicians. Ray saw an audition as the opportunity he had been waiting for, a way to get out of Florida and travel the country.

Ray Charles arrived at the club, ready to prove himself. Millinder had no time to waste and got right to the point. "Let's see what you got," he said.

Ray played the piano and sang several songs, numbers he had been performing for the past two years. When he finished, he felt good and waited for Millinder's response.

"Sorry, kid," said the noted bandleader. "You ain't good enough."

Shocked, Ray stammered, "W-w-w-what?"

Millinder was blunt with his reply. "You heard me. You don't got what it takes."

Ray felt like he had been hit over the head with a sledgehammer. He could not believe his ears. *"You don't got what it takes."* No one had ever said those words to him before. Ray was used to compliments. Everyone was always praising his playing and singing. Yet here he was, playing for the first truly renowned musician he had ever met, someone known from coast to coast, and this man completely rejected him. Ray was crushed.

But Ray was also determined—and he was stubborn. No doubt his feelings had been hurt by Lucky Millinder, who not only had criticized him but had offered no words of encouragement whatsoever. At the same time, Ray trusted his own ears. He compared himself to the musicians he heard on records. Through records, he knew the giants of jazz: tenor saxophonists Coleman Hawkins, Lester Young, and Illinois Jacquet; alto saxophonists Charlie Parker, Benny Carter, and Johnny Hodges; trumpeters Roy Eldridge, Dizzy Gillespie, and Buck Clayton; guitarist Charlie Christian; bassist Oscar Pettiford; and pianists Teddy Wilson and Erroll Garner. At age 17, Ray Charles realized he was not yet in their class. These artists were the masters of the music. Yet as Ray played throughout Florida in many different combos and big bands, he knew that he was as capable as most of his colleagues. Beyond that, he knew he was improving. Although Ray had few gigs and little money, he had ironclad tenacity. In his heart he had a burning desire to make it, to expand his horizons. Consequently, when a trip with the Joe Anderson band led to Tampa, he decided to put Orlando behind him and move on. He was ready to experience a new city.

He might not have been prepared to live in a Tampa flophouse, but that is where he started out. Several categories below a hotel, this was a place where, for a dime a night, everyone just flopped on the floor of a big room, sometimes sleeping on blankets or, if they were lucky, discarded mattresses. Living conditions quickly improved, however, when Ray met guitarist Gosady McGee, who introduced Ray to two sisters who were acquaintances of his. The women, Freddie and Lydia, took a liking to Ray and invited him to stay in their house. He was delighted about their invitation, especially when he learned that the sisters had a piano in their living room.

Gradually, work came Ray's way. Charlie Brantley hired him for a gig. Brantley was such an avid fan of Louis Jordan's that, according to Ray, "he sounded like he ate Jordan's records for breakfast."

When Brantley's gig ended, Ray found work as the third of a trio, led by drummer Manzy Harris and complemented by bassist Otto McQueen. This group copied the instrumentation of the King Cole Trio, which had become more popular than ever, and it provided the perfect setting for Ray's singing and playing in the Nat Cole and Charles Brown styles.

Ray never felt guilty about imitating Nat Cole. He considered emulating Cole to be a challenge, and he had it down to a science. Cole was his idol, and Ray modeled his own music after Cole's as a tribute to the musician he most admired. Besides, Cole's music and vocal style were what

paying customers wanted to hear, songs like "Route 66" and "I Can't See for Lookin'."

Ray's most bizarre job during the late 1940s was with the Florida Playboys; it was peculiar because the Playboys were a white hillbilly band. Ray's musical versatility saw him through, though, and he fit right in with the steel guitars and fiddles that played the country hits of the day, such as "Anytime" and "Kentucky Waltz." Ray even learned how to yodel. Although racial segregation in the South was practiced as severely as ever, audiences accepted Ray Charles as a member of the white group. Furthermore, there were no racial incidents in the white

From left to right: *Music greats Max Kaminsky (Dixieland), Lester Young (swing), "Hot Lips" Page (swing), Charlie Parker (bebop), and Lennie Tristano (cool) appear together for a show at the opening of New York City's Birdland restaurant in 1949. Ray often compared himself to the masters of jazz he heard on records, but at age 17 he realized he was not yet in their class.*

clubs where the Florida Playboys performed, perhaps because Ray rendered country-and-western music with as much feeling as any other southerner.

Meanwhile, Ray had not abandoned playing the blues, nor would he ever. In fact, the first recording he ever made was a blues number sung into a primitive wire recorder that an acquaintance had brought over to Freddie and Lydia's house. Ray composed the song and called it "I Found My Baby There" (also known as "St. Pete's Blues") and today it is still available on compilations of Charles's early work. At only 17 years of age, Ray had the voice of a much older man—deep, soulful, and filled with adult pain.

In truth, Ray had become an adult at an early age. He had his first serious love affair in Tampa, and even though the words to "I Found My Baby There" indicate that he discovered love in "St. Pete, Florida," the actual location was Tampa. His lover's name was Louise, and she was Ray's age. Louise was intelligent and pretty. He liked the sound of her voice and she admired his talent. The couple became virtually inseparable. Louise attended Ray's gigs and spent all her afternoons and evenings with him. She found him fascinating; he found her irresistible. Their temperaments matched and their sense of humor was in perfect sync. After a few months, they decided to live together.

Louise's parents, however, did not approve of the relationship. To begin with, they did not like the idea of their daughter living with a musician—a blind musician with an uncertain future. Yet the more they protested, the more rebellious she became. Consequently, when Ray, who had saved some money from his gigs with the Playboys, suggested that they run off to Miami, Louise did not object.

After a few months of living together in Miami, however, the pressure from Louise's parents for her to return to Tampa proved too much for the couple. Louise agreed to move back, but only with the condition that she could continue to live with Ray. Ray and Louise found a room for three dollars a week in a woman's house in West Tampa, and for a few more months, life was peaceful. Ray found work in a white club and was happy being with Louise, but he grew restless in his professional life.

Ray had always wanted to expand his horizons. Before he went to sleep at night, he often fantasized, dreaming about the rest of the country and about living in faraway cities like New York, Chicago, and Los Angeles. He sought new experiences. He did not like the idea of never having ventured farther than a few hundred miles from his hometown of Greensville.

One day when Ray's friend, guitarist Gosady McGee, came to visit Ray and Louise, Ray asked McGee to bring a map of the United States. "Take that map," Ray told McGee, "and put your finger on Tampa." McGee did what his friend asked. "Now," Ray continued, "find the biggest city furthest away from here. Go as far as you possibly can without leaving America." McGee slid his finger across the map, all the way up to the state of Washington. (Alaska did not become a U.S. state until 1959.)

"Looks like the furthest point from here is the city of Seattle, Washington," said McGee.

"Good," said Ray, "'cause that's where I'm going."

The McSon Trio, with Ray on piano, Gosady McGee on guitar, and Milt Garred on bass, was modeled after the King Cole Trio. The McSon Trio landed a gig at the Rocking Chair, a popular club on 14th and Yesler in Seattle, Washington.

4

COAST TO COAST

THE JOURNEY TO SEATTLE was rugged. By Greyhound bus, the trip took five days and five nights. The roads were bumpy and there was nothing to do on the bus. Ray traveled alone. He was sad about leaving Louise, but it was something he had to do. He was also excited about his future; at 18, he decided to change his life.

When the bus finally pulled into the deserted Seattle bus station, it was the middle of the night. Someone directed Ray to a cheap hotel where he slept for 24 hours. When he awoke, he felt disoriented, a little confused, and extremely hungry. It was night, and he asked directions to a restaurant. At such a late hour, he was told, the only place open was a nightclub called the Rocking Chair. Ray caught a cab.

A beefy bouncer stood at the door and said, "Sorry, kid, you're too young to get in here. It's Talent Night, but you gotta be 21."

"Talent night!" Ray exclaimed. "Look, I gotta get in. I got a talent. I'm a musician."

"You're underage," the bouncer replied.

"Let me in for just a second," Ray pleaded. "You'll hear me sing. I play piano, too. You'll see I'm not jiving you."

"You better not be," said the bouncer as he opened the door for Charles and then led him to the stage.

A couple of singers, a sax player, and an exotic dancer were to perform that evening. Ray patiently waited until they had finished performing before he was directed to the piano. For the next few minutes, while his stomach groaned with hunger, he concentrated on the music as he delivered two of his favorite numbers, "Traveling Blues" and "Drifting Blues," in his perfected Charles Brown style. The lyrics reflected Ray's own nomadic condition and he sang with uncompromising emotion. The crowd loved him.

After he completed his songs and the applause died down, a man touched Ray on the arm. "Pretty good," he said. "You wouldn't be interested in forming a little trio and playing over at the Elks' Club, would you?"

"Would I!" cried Ray.

"Well, be there Friday night. And be on time. You'll start at nine," said the Elks' Club manager.

The Elks' Club gig worked out. Not long after Ray arrived in Seattle, he was joined by Gosady McGee and bassist Milt Garred. They formed the McSon Trio (the "Mc" came from McGee and "Son," from Robinson). This was also the time when Ray decided to drop his last name, Robinson, and simply use Ray Charles. The celebrated boxer Sugar Ray Robinson had already made a name for himself, and Charles later said, "I figured that two Ray Robinsons might be one too many."

The years 1948–49 in Seavttle were productive professionally for Ray Charles. He began to write more original compositions, such as "The Snow Is Falling," which reflected his attitude about the cold, wet climate, and "The

Rocking Chair," a blues word-picture about the nightclub he had played at when he first came to town.

Charles modeled the McSon Trio after the King Cole Trio. Charles's fascination with Nat Cole had only intensified and he had now mastered Cole's form. In addition, Charles developed his skills as a big-band arranger, having been deeply influenced by the daringly new bebop style of modern orchestras led by Dizzy Gillespie, Woody Herman, and Stan Kenton, as well as the popular rocking rhythm bands like Lionel Hampton's.

The Rocking Chair, the club Ray went to the night after arriving in Seattle, hosted a talent night that evening, and Ray talked himself into the place so that he could perform for the customers there. Ray later wrote a song, "Rocking Chair Blues," in honor of the club.

The black Elks' Club, located on Jackson Street, had a nightclub on the second floor. Ray played his first gig in Seattle at the Elks' Club.

In Seattle, Charles also met a trumpet player, Quincy Jones, who was a few years younger than Charles. Charles became Jones's mentor, teaching him how to write for a big band. Jones came to be Charles's lifelong friend and would eventually become one of the most celebrated arranger-producers of jazz and pop music, later producing some of singer Michael Jackson's biggest hits.

After only a month in Seattle, Ray had saved enough money to send for Louise. Her parents protested vehemently, but Louise was determined to rejoin him. She made the long cross-country trip, and she and Ray soon set up housekeeping together again. Their relationship was sometimes smooth, sometimes rough. For the most part, Charles was devoted to Louise, although occasionally he had other girlfriends. Because they were still teenagers and because neither of them had ever lived away from Florida, they were often emotionally on edge. Louise's parents, especially her mother, kept up the pressure, calling, writing, and pleading with Louise to return home. Ray went for long periods of time without finding work and the lack of money added to the tense situation. Louise and Ray were in love, but they were learning that it takes a lot more than love to keep a relationship together.

The most pressing matter on Charles's mind was his music, not his romance. To Charles's delight and amazement, Jack Lauderdale, the owner of Down Beat (later called Swing Time) record label, had heard him play at the Rocking Chair and had asked the McSon Trio to cut a record. On one side of the 78-rpm recording they played "Confession Blues," written by Charles, and on the other, "I Love You, I Love You," composed by Joe Lee Lawrence, Charles's school friend from his days in St. Augustine. During the 1940s, records were manufactured in the form of thick, breakable shellac, called 78s because they turned at a fast 78 revolutions per minute.

Lauderdale liked Charles's vocals and piano playing and asked him to come to Los Angeles, California, to record—not with the members of the McSon Trio, but with the musicians Oscar and Johnny Moore, who had played with Charles's idols, Nat Cole and Charles Brown. Out of the Los Angeles session came "Baby, Let Me Hold Your Hand," which proved to be Ray's first record to become a national hit. The music charts, or listings, like so many aspects of American life at the time, were segregated, the black music from the white. (In the 1940s, black music was categorized as "Race Records," which was changed to "Rhythm and Blues" in 1949.) Charles was thrilled to know his song was being bought and played on jukeboxes throughout black America. His financial situation, however, improved little. At this point in his career, Ray did not receive royalties from the music he wrote or recorded. No one had ever explained to him how to register for a copyright on his compositions, thereby establishing the sole legal right to reproduce, publish, and sell his work.

It was also during this period that Charles began to use hard drugs. Illegal drug use in the late 1940s was especially widespread among musicians. Taking drugs was fashionable but harmful, and in some cases, the deadly effects of

Guitarist Oscar Moore was one of the musicians with whom Jack Lauderdale of Swing Time records had asked Ray to record in the late 1940s. From 1939 to 1944, Moore had played in the King Cole Trio, which produced such big hits as "Straighten Up and Fly Right."

certain drugs were not widely understood. Smoking marijuana and sniffing and injecting heroin were commonplace. Although Ray Charles does not believe that smoking marijuana led him to taking heroin, he wound up using both.

"I was curious," Charles later recalled. "Just as I had been curious about music and mechanics, I was also curious about drugs. I knew the boys were doing it, and I bugged them until they gave me some. There was no pusher who hung around the back alley enticing me. No white cat or black cat got me hooked or encouraged me to turn on. Whatever I did, I take sole responsibility for."

Ray Charles was 18 years old when he started his drug habit, a habit that would last about 16 years. Meanwhile, his relationship with Louise was breaking up. Louise's mother finally got her way, and toward the end of 1949 she sent her daughter a ticket, demanding that she return home. Louise and Ray were heartbroken, but the strain of living in Seattle turned out to be too great for them; they fought all the time. Louise left Seattle, and five weeks later, lonely and ready for another change, Ray and his McSon Trio traveled to Los Angeles to record.

Soon after returning to Tampa, Louise learned that she was pregnant with Ray's child. But when she tried to contact Ray in Seattle, he had already headed south to California without leaving a forwarding address. She did not know how to get in touch with him, and in 1950, Louise and Ray's daughter, Evelyn, was born. Ray eventually found out about his daughter, acknowledging and supporting her from the beginning. Although Louise and Ray remained friends, Louise ultimately married someone else.

By 1950, Charles's life took another dramatic turn. He made a permanent move to Los Angeles. His reputation was growing, especially after "Baby, Let Me Hold Your Hand" became a hit. As a result of the burgeoning defense and airplane industries, jobs were plentiful in southern

California. Manufacturers employed blacks in greater numbers than ever before. It was also a time of intense musical activity in Los Angeles, and Charles found himself in the middle of it. Nat "King" Cole was hotter than ever; postwar bebop, with its brilliant complexities, was the rage; and the blues—especially Texas blues as rendered by electric guitarist–singer T-Bone Walker—were also fashionable. Louis Jordan and a flock of his imitators were wildly popular, and rhythm and blues, the name for the new black dance music, was in vogue. The older, more traditional jazz artists, such as Art Tatum, were still active, too. (One evening in Los Angeles, Ray actually got to meet the great pianist Art Tatum, the musician whom Charles and his colleagues most admired and whom they referred to as "God." Awestruck when he shook Tatum's hand, Charles could not utter a word to his idol.)

Jack Lauderdale, owner of the Swing Time label, proved to be more interested in Charles as a solo artist than as a member of the McSon Trio. The trio recorded a few more songs for Swing Time, including "Honey, Honey" and "She's on the Ball," but the group found few opportunities to perform live. It was at this time that Charles met Loretta, Lauderdale's secretary, and she became Ray's girlfriend. Charles moved into her cottage and, in typical style, found a way to survive in a new city, while Milt Garred and Gosady McGee returned to Seattle.

Lauderdale had big plans for Ray. He wanted to broaden Charles's audience by seeking national exposure for him. Cutting records helped, but Ray needed to tour. Because Charles was not known well enough to draw a crowd on his own, he teamed up with another Swing Time artist, Lowell Fulson, a blues singer-guitarist whose "Every Day I Have the Blues" was a smash hit in black neighborhoods across the country. Charles toured nationwide for $35 a night, playing piano in Fulson's band and doing a 10-minute set of his own material. He also wrote some of Fulson's arrangements.

For the first time in his life, Ray traveled with a big-time band, touring throughout Texas, into the Deep South, up the East Coast to New York, and then west to Chicago. Along the way, he met and, if occasion demanded, played behind some of the greatest artists of the day, including T-Bone Walker and Big Joe Turner, and gospel singing groups like the Dixie Hummingbirds, the Five Blind Boys, and the Swan Silvertones. A man with a spirited and spontaneous sense of humor, Ray enjoyed laughing as he often shared the billing with the great comics of the day, such as Jackie "Moms" Mabley, Redd Foxx, and Pigmeat Markham. Charles's old friend, Quincy Jones, was playing trumpet with Lionel Hampton's big band at the time, and when their paths crossed, Jones and Charles always found time to jam.

Along with the excitement of being on the road, there was also anguish and humiliation. Sleeping facilities in most cities were segregated. The musicians were forced to find black-only living accommodations, and if none were available, they looked for rooming houses or for rooms in private homes. There were times when the musicians slept in the car. Charles heard about signs posted in some small towns that read NO NIGGERS, JEWS, OR DOGS ALLOWED.

Charles maintained his heroin habit with the money he saved from his gigs. Always a tireless and conscientious worker, Charles had a rare ability to perform, and at times even excel, in spite of the dangerous narcotic he shot into his arm. His fast-paced world never slowed down for a second.

Even though Charles was slow to change his musical style—he always wanted to be sure that what he played pleased the public and ensured his financial survival—he remained true to his own artistic taste. For years he had performed his versions of Nat Cole's and Charles Brown's songs. His small hit records, his own trios, the inflection of his voice, and even the nature of his compositions were all set in that easy-listening, jazzy, cool California mold.

But people began to ask Charles about his own musical style. Charles experimented, singing in a voice that was more natural, not imitative of anyone else, a voice that more genuinely expressed his own emotions. He was not yet ready to record in that voice, but he soon would be.

Never lacking excitement in his life, Ray Charles had more girlfriends, traveled continually, and in 1951, bought his first car, a used Rocket Ninety-eight Oldsmobile. A pal drove for him, and many times Charles repaired the engine himself. He still loved mechanical gadgets and bought a shortwave radio, which he could also fix. After playing in Atlanta, Georgia, he rode to Greensville to visit his old friends, who were impressed by his rising fame and his

Ray plays with an early band in Texas in the 1950s. David "Fathead" Newman (far left), on baritone saxophone, was an accomplished jazz musician and became one of Ray's closest friends.

records that played on the radio. It was during this time that, much to everyone's surprise, Charles got married.

The marriage was short-lived and, in some ways, an unusually impetuous move for a man who was frequently cautious. Through his friend Billy Brooks, a trumpeter in Lowell Fulson's band, Charles met Eileen, a beautician in Columbus, Ohio. Charles had been impressed by Billy's marriage, and the more Ray thought about it, the more he liked the idea of starting a family of his own. He proposed to Eileen, she accepted, and they were married. But the relationship did not have much of a chance to succeed, considering Charles's grueling touring schedule.

Two months into the marriage, Ray decided to leave Lowell Fulson's band and tour as a single act. He felt it was the right time to go solo, even though he would be gone from home much of the time. Charles was also having difficulty in accepting Eileen's drinking. He admitted to himself and to his friends that his attitude about alcohol seemed hypocritical—after all, he himself was using hard drugs—but he was nonetheless intolerant of women who drank heavily. The relationship fell apart after only 18 months.

The year 1952 represented enormous changes in Charles's life. He not only decided to go out on his own—he was too self-confident to continue as a sideman—but he was also signed by the Shaw Agency, a powerful organization that found him more lucrative bookings. Most critical of all the changes, however, was switching record labels—he had outgrown the small Swing Time label, and Atlantic Records, located in New York City, expressed an interest in him. Changing labels, along with his declaration of independence as a solo artist, would dramatically alter the course of Ray Charles's career and the future of American music.

When Ray decided to become a solo performer, his salary jumped from about $50 per night (with Lowell Fulson's band) to $75 per night.

5

CHANGING SOUNDS

RAY CHARLES MADE STEADY progress in his career. With Lowell Fulson, he had made $50 a night. As a solo performer, the amount jumped to $70 or $75. Charles had a few minor hits, such as "Kissa Me, Baby," with his former label, and at Atlantic, at least for the first few years, he would continue to have modest success.

Ray was living in New York, in a Harlem hotel on 126th Street and Eighth Avenue, when Atlantic owners Herb Abramson and Ahmet Ertegun came to talk to him about cutting records with them. They had heard his "Baby, Let Me Hold Your Hand" and liked the song. Abramson and Ertegun bought Charles's contract from Jack Lauderdale for $2,500. The Atlantic label, founded in 1948, was small compared with firms like Columbia and Decca, but it was a larger company than Swing Time. Atlantic's specialty was producing black music aimed at black listeners. Charles received little money up front in the deal—he would

Left to right: *Atlantic Records executive Jerry Wexler, singers Ruth Brown, Clyde McPhatter, and Lavern Baker, and Atlantic Records founder Ahmet Ertegun pose for a photograph in the 1950s. Ray signed a contract with Atlantic and toured as a backup singer for Ruth Brown, a successful rhythm-and-blues singer.*

have to continue to count on live performances for his bread and butter—but felt comfortable with Abramson and Ertegun, who, in addition to being astute businessmen, were sincere and knowledgeable music lovers. Their label had already enjoyed success with rhythm-and-blues singers Ruth Brown and Joe Turner.

Ray's first records for Atlantic were still stylistically linked to his past. He had not completely abandoned his Charles Brown/Nat Cole routine, as is evident in such songs as "Funny, But I Still Love You." On other early Atlantic releases one can hear the emergence of a Ray Charles who is raw and more distinctly individual. "Mess Around," a song written by Ahmet Ertegun, is an early example of Ray Charles sounding like himself. His voice is not as pretty or smooth as Nat Cole's, but it is far more rhythmic and openly emotional. Atlantic provided the backup band and the musical arrangements, but this, too, would change.

Ray Charles's struggle for financial survival on the road continued. To keep going, he agreed to play piano for trumpeter Joe Morris, another Atlantic artist, whose "Anytime, Anyplace, Anywhere" became a national hit in 1951. When he was not backing up Morris, Charles proceeded to work solo, using pickup bands as he traveled from city to city. Trying to obtain musicians while on tour drove Charles crazy. Because he was a perfectionist, Ray could not tolerate wrong notes or sloppy playing. Finally, after a painful episode in Philadelphia, Pennsylvania, where his makeshift band was especially incompetent, Charles made up his mind to accomplish something he had long dreamed of doing: forming his own band.

Charles finally achieved his dream in Texas. By the mid-1950s, he was living in Dallas, the home base for his first band. In Dallas, Ray met David "Fathead" Newman, a brilliant saxophonist, who would become one of Ray's closest friends and musical associates. Like Charles, Newman was a technically accomplished jazz player. Charles's theory was that if he built his band around skilled jazz musicians, other aspects—the less demanding blues and rhythm-and-blues styles—would then come easily. His first group was a septet: two saxes, two trumpets, a piano, a bass, and drums. Ray Charles sometimes doubled up on alto sax, giving the band three saxes when needed. He wrote all the arrangements and he had the knack of making 7 pieces sound like 14. Thrilled that he was finally a leader with the ability to form and control his musical environment, Ray Charles decided that he would never again be without his own band.

In 1955, Charles met a woman in Texas who soon became his second wife. Della, whom he called B after her middle name, Beatrice, was a gospel singer from Houston. She was a quiet, bright woman whose soft manner captured Ray's heart. He also liked the fact that, as a churchgoing woman, she neither smoked nor drank alcohol.

With a new wife and a new band, Ray Charles was, indeed, ready to move forward. He toured as the backup for Ruth Brown, whose "Mama, He Treats Your Daughter

Mean" was a smash hit on the black music charts. Still in his early twenties, Charles was about to enter what many consider to be the most productive and significant period of his creative life. He was on the verge of creating musical innovations that would be felt throughout the world for decades to come.

It began as a practical matter. Charles did not always like the songs that were sent to him by Atlantic executive Ahmet Ertegun or Ertegun's new partner, Jerry Wexler. As a result, he began writing more original material. And because he had a band at his disposal, one that reflected his individuality, Charles finally had all the musical resources at his command to create inventive pieces. He could experiment, write on the road, and test out the material before live audiences. As a writer, arranger, and performer, he could express the fullness of his personality. He could go back—back before bebop or swing or the smooth stylings of Nat Cole—back to the two musical strains he had heard first as a small child: gospel and blues.

At the Shiloh Baptist Church in Greensville, Ray had learned traditional spirituals and gospel songs passed down through the generations, folk material of intense emotions and hand-clapping hot rhythms. In the church of Ray's youth, the fervent parishioners danced in the aisle. So when Ray came to forge his own form of dance music, he utilized those spirituals, sometimes retaining the rhythms and melodies while changing the lyrics. "My Lord" became "my baby." A religious number like "You Better Leave That Liar Alone," sung in Ray's blues-inflected voice, was transformed into "You Better Leave That Woman Alone." For perhaps the first time in American popular music, the fiery intensity of the African-American country church was translated into sexy, secular terms.

Not everyone was pleased about this transformation. Charles was called sacrilegious by ministers. From

A montage of photographs of various musicians who appeared at New York City's renowned Apollo Theater (top right) include images of David "Fathead" Newman (top left, center, and bottom left—with singer Mary Ann Fisher) and Ray Charles at the piano (bottom right). Charles's first band was a septet: two saxes (one of which was played by Newman), two trumpets, Ray's piano, a bass, and drums.

their pulpits, a few preachers verbally attacked him, but Charles did not allow their condemnation to affect him. He felt both comfortable and honest utilizing this material from his past. To him, all music could be merged and mixed. Now, after so many years of imitating others, his voice—his overall musical conception—was completely his own. To make matters even more satisfying for Ray, the public liked his new blend of gospel blues. "I Got a Woman" was his first important number rendered in this style, and the song, which Ray wrote in 1954, elevated his career to a new plateau. It was released in 1955 and became a smash hit on the rhythm-and-blues chart.

Charles continued to travel, touring the country with his seven- or eight-piece band, playing raunchy nightclubs, dives, and an occasional outdoor concert. From the mid- to the late 1950s he surrounded himself with superb musicians, including saxophonists Donald Wilkerson and Leroy "Hog" Cooper, trumpeters Marcus Belgrave and Phil Guilbeau, bassist Edgar Willis, and especially baritone and alto saxophonist Hank Crawford, who collaborated with Charles on arrangements and eventually became his bandleader.

The last half of the decade also saw the birth of rock and roll, a white version of rhythm and blues. Charles was an important part of this phenomenon. White artists often did their own versions of a song, called covers, usually making far more money than black artists who sang the original songs. Singer Pat Boone, for example, covered many rhythm-and-blues numbers by Little Richard and Fats Domino, outearning the original artists. The same was true for Georgia Gibbs's 1955 sanitized version of Etta James's earthy "Roll with Me Henry." Likewise, Ray's early successes were recorded by many, including Elvis Presley and pop-jazz singer Peggy Lee.

Ray's hits came quickly: "A Fool for You" (1955); "Drown In My Own Tears," "Hallelujah, I Love Her So," and "Lonely Avenue" (1956); "Swanee River Rock" (1957); "Yes Indeed" (1958); and "The Right Time" (1959). The dramatic difference in these recordings was that, unlike his early sessions for Atlantic, Ray Charles was in charge. Most artists of the time were directed by others; Charles, however, was his own producer, arranger, and, frequently, songwriter. The Atlantic staff was astute to allow Ray to be the master of his music.

Unlike his fellow pioneers of groundbreaking rhythm and blues, Charles did not direct his music at teenagers. In contrast, the songs of Chuck Berry were deliberately aimed at white youth; the lyrics of Berry's "Sweet Sixteen" or "Almost Grown," for instance, speak directly to that market. Ray Charles's music, like his old-beyond-his-years voice, was mature, its subject matter addressed adults rather than young people. Nonetheless, with "What I Say," his megahit of 1959, he won over black and white audiences alike. This irresistibly spirited, highly sexual song had a call-and-response pattern that echoed the rapport between preacher and congregation that Charles had heard in his childhood church. No cover version of "What

I Say" approached the popularity of Charles's original recording.

"What I Say" was Ray Charles's first Top 10 song on both the white and black charts, making him, at long last, a national star. Before this hit, however, two musical developments had enriched and expanded his personality even further. The first was the addition of women to his musical ensemble. When the band was first formed, Charles had employed Mary Ann Fisher as a featured vocalist. He liked the feeling of a female voice backing up his own. At the end of 1955, when he recorded "Drown in My Own Tears," he wanted more of that feeling, so he employed additional female singers to give the song a church-choir sound. By 1957, with several hits under his belt, he was ready to make women's voices a permanent part of his sound. He listened to a group of three young singers called the Cookies, Margie Hendrix, Darlene Mac-Rae, and Pat Mosley, whom he hired and renamed the Raeletts. Margie Hendrix, the leader, was an especially powerful vocalist who sang with an expressive, rough-hewn voice reminiscent of Charles's. A brilliant example of Hendrix's artistry can be heard on two albums, reissued as *Ray Charles, Live* on the Atlantic label—a recording of the 1958 Newport Jazz Festival and a 1959 concert in Atlanta, Georgia. Hendrix's solos on "The Right Time" and "Tell the Truth" are emotional firestorms.

Charles's heralded performance at the 1958 Newport Jazz Festival introduced the second development of his musical personality—his continuing concentration on jazz. Alone among the 1950s rhythm-and-blues (R & B) artists who directly influenced the development of rock and roll, Ray Charles retained his status as a sophisticated jazz musician, even in the midst of his popularity as a maker of commercial dance tunes. His band could play both styles, R & B and jazz; they could play burning bebop as in "Hot Rod" or down-and-out, up-to-the-minute blues as in "A Fool for You."

During the 1950s, record companies started to produce long-playing albums (LPs). Previously, there were only singles—single records with two songs, one on each side. When the album form was born, albums were merely compilations of single songs. But by the mid-1950s, albums began to reflect an overall concept, an hour or more of music created in one sustained mood. Along these lines, Nesuhi Ertegun, the older brother of Atlantic Records president Ahmet Ertegun and head of the company's jazz department, asked Charles to play with the leading jazz artists of the day. Many of these mellow jazz records, especially those recorded with vibraphonist Milt Jackson (*Soul Brothers* in 1958 and *Soul Meeting* in 1962) are considered classics, proving Charles's ability, beyond that of a popular singer, as a first-rate instrumentalist. Quincy Jones, Charles's friend from Seattle who by now had emerged as a prominent producer, arranged several of these sessions.

Critics and fans referred to Ray Charles as a genius, although he, himself, was not comfortable with the term. "To me," he later said, "Art Tatum was a genius, not me. I didn't want to feel compelled to live up to the name. I didn't want to be called a genius. Just R. C. Or Brother Ray." Still others called him the Bishop, the Right Reverend, or the High Priest of Soul.

The Genius of Ray Charles, an Atlantic album from 1959, became a career landmark. Produced by Nesuhi Ertegun and Jerry Wexler, this was yet another departure for the singer. The first side contained a series of big-band numbers with members of Count Basie's orchestra. Songs like "Let the Good Times Roll," arranged by Quincy Jones, reminded Charles of the 1940s and his love of Louis Jordan. Side two was devoted to ballads backed by a full string section. This was a first for Ray; never before had he sung over violins. He relished the experience and interpreted the love songs "Just for a Thrill," "Am I Blue?" and "Come Rain or Come Shine" with extreme tenderness, joining a select company of singers, such as Louis Armstrong, Billie Holiday, and Dinah Washington, in being able to infuse a bittersweet blues feeling into nonblues material. The album was a triumph.

Ray Charles's world underwent a radical change. Only a few years earlier he had played the segregated South, refusing dates where African Americans were forced to sit in the balcony. Now, in 1959, he played New York City's Carnegie Hall, home to the world's most respected classical musicians. Through a series of remarkably diverse recordings—R & B hits, jazz dates, and big-band and ballad sessions—he had not only gained a varied and large audience but had won the respect of fellow musicians and critics alike. At age 29, Ray Charles had become a cultural hero, a figure who, through both ingenious and natural means, had nourished his music of the present with the rich roots of his past. He was credited with inventing soul music and starting a trend in jazz that stressed the music's churchy, country origins. But beyond the celebrity and praise he received, Charles still had some difficulties to confront. Although Ray Charles would witness even greater achievements during the 1960s, he would suffer greater anguish.

Jazz musician Milt Jackson plays the vibraphone in New York in 1950. Charles and Jackson cut two jazz records together with Atlantic, Soul Brothers *in 1958 and* Soul Meeting *in 1962, both of which became classic recordings*

In 1962, Charles, wearing his trademark sunglasses, is seen here reading music in braille at a recording studio.

6

SUCCESS AND STRESS

RAY CHARLES AND HIS WIFE DELLA had three sons: Ray junior was born in 1956, David arrived in 1958, and Bobby in 1961. The Charles family had moved from Dallas to Los Angeles, and the marriage, although difficult, managed to survive until 1975, when Ray and Della were divorced. Della had been extremely patient with Ray. He once described himself as "wild when it comes to females," and he would not change his ways. In 1959, he and the Raelett Margie Hendrix had a son and named him Charles Wayne. There were four other instances when Charles would father children outside of his marriage; in two of these cases he became involved in paternity suits. Charles never denied fathering the children or refused financial help to the mother and child; however, he did argue over what he considered to be excessive alimony or child-support payments.

The other source of chaos in his personal life concerned narcotics. In 1958, he was arrested for drug possession in Philadelphia, Pennsylvania; in 1961, the police raided his hotel room in Indianapolis, Indiana, and found heroin. In both cases, through the help of expert lawyers, Charles was acquitted. "Just like you can buy grades of silk," he later remarked about his legal battles, "you can buy grades of justice. I was lucky. I had the money to get good attorneys." Despite these arrests, however, Charles stubbornly continued to use drugs. "The only person I was hurting," he later said, "was me. I knew the stuff was poison. When I didn't have enough heroin I'd get sick like every other junkie. But I figured that was my business and no one else's."

Ray is questioned by Indianapolis police after his arrest on a narcotics charge on November 14, 1961. Despite his arrest and acquittal, Ray continued to use heroin until he admitted himself into a hospital in 1965.

Meanwhile, his music did not seem to suffer any side effects from his drug habit. If anything, Charles grew more popular with the public. In 1959, he changed labels, switching to ABC Records, a company whose roster included more mainstream artists than Atlantic's. Moreover, ABC offered Charles higher royalties and, most significant, ownership of the masters of all of his recordings, a move that would earn him millions of dollars later in his career. After a decade of hard-nosed experience on the road and of dealing with all types of promoters, Charles had become a shrewd businessman. He changed personal managers, switching from longtime friend Jeff Brown to Joe Adams, a former Los Angeles disc jockey and seasoned professional who would run Ray Charles's organization with ironclad discipline for the next three decades.

In 1960, Ray Charles and his octet (he added a saxophonist) went to Europe for the first time. They had a large following there and were affectionately welcomed by the public. The love affair between Ray and his overseas fans would only intensify through the years. After his return to the States, Charles continued to record with the small group. Songs recorded for ABC, such as "Sticks and Stones" (1960), "Unchain My Heart" (1961), and "Hit the Road, Jack" (1961), became huge hits as Ray stayed with the strong gospel-soul sound he had first developed on the Atlantic label. He also cut a big-band jazz album, called *Genius Plus Soul Equals Jazz,* which was released in 1961 and enjoyed tremendous popularity. It also produced a hit single, entitled "One Mint Julep," a rare feat for a jazz album.

More confident than ever, Charles decided that the time was right to take the one musical step he had been dreaming about for years: to form a big band. Ever since he heard the big bands of Benny Goodman, Count Basie, and Duke Ellington as a child, the sound of 16 or 17 instruments playing together had excited him. He wanted a big band

Ray signs a contract with Sam Clarke of ABC Records in 1959. ABC offered Ray higher royalties for his music than Atlantic had and ownership of the masters of all of his recordings.

that would not only project excellence on its own, but provide the ideal background for his singing. In the fall of 1961, using his small band as the base and Hank Crawford as musical director, Charles employed five saxes, four trumpets, four trombones, and a rhythm section in which his piano was the anchor.

Economically, creating the big band was not a profitable move. The overhead for a big band is huge, and just as many people would have paid to see Ray Charles with a small group. But his desire to feel that musical muscle behind him was more important than money; the sheer power of the brass and saxes gave him a kick. Never again would Ray Charles tour without his own big band as backup.

A year earlier, in 1960, Ray Charles broke still more new ground. He had the first number-one-across-the-board record of his career. His interpretation of "Georgia on My Mind," a song written in 1930 by Hoagy Carmichael, raced to the top of virtually every music popularity chart in the United States, proving to be Charles's biggest crossover hit to date. (*Crossover* is the term the music industry uses when an artist from a smaller category, such as rhythm and blues, achieves popularity among a broader, predominantly white audience.) Charles's rendition of the song, complete with large orchestra and violins, is considered by most to be a masterpiece; he was able to transform what had been a mainstream melody into a lament from his own dark past. He shaped the material to fit his own emotional needs and the results touched every listener.

Later in the year Charles enjoyed another hit in the same mode, "Ruby," a poignant ballad in which his voice was complemented by a large string section. In 1961, he recorded a brilliant record of duets with bebop vocalist Betty

Ray listens to ABC recordings with arrangers Sid Feller (center) and Gerald Wilson in 1961. With their gospel-soul style, "Unchain My Heart" and "Hit the Road, Jack" became huge hits for Ray and ABC in 1961.

Carter, entitled *Ray Charles and Betty Carter.* Some of the duets included on the album are "You and I," "People Will Say We're in Love," and "Baby, It's Cold Outside."

Ray Charles had, indeed, come a long way since recording "I Found My Baby There" on a crude tape recorder in Tampa, Florida. In 14 years, he had become one of the most beloved performers in America and Europe. He was earning big money, enough to buy his own airplane. His me-

chanical curiosity intact, he learned all he could about the twin-engine plane, a Cessna 310, and even taught himself to make minor engine repairs.

Once, on a flight out of New Mexico, the tower cleared Ray's plane for 11,000 feet through some mountainous terrain. That figure sounded wrong to Charles, who always sat next to the pilot and monitored every aspect of the operation. Charles suggested that the pilot check the flight

Ray Charles, the Raeletts, and the Ray Charles Band perform in the early 1960s. In 1961, Ray decided to form a big band to add musical muscle behind his vocals; he would never again tour without one as backup.

In the 1960s, Ray poses with Raeletts (clockwise, from top) Merry Clayton, Clydie King, Alex Brown, and Gwen Berry. Ray Charles was the most popular singer in the nation before Beatlemania and the rise of Motown in 1964.

plan, and consequently they discovered that the tower had made a mistake; clearance should have been set at 13,000 feet. If Charles had not sensed the error, the plane might have crashed into the side of a mountain.

In 1962, his confidence building, Ray Charles made another decision that, to almost everyone else, seemed wrongheaded, even crazy. He was determined to sing country-and-western songs—in fact, he wanted to make an entire album of country music.

ABC Records tried to dissuade Charles, but he did not budge. For well over a decade he had been producing and directing his own sound; he knew what he wanted. "People won't accept you singing hillbilly songs," an expert argued. "Your old fans will desert you and country music fans will resent you."

But Charles saw it differently; he was determined to sing certain songs that, like rhythm and blues and popular ballads, had been an integral part of his childhood. Those hours spent listening to the "Grand Ole Opry" as a boy back in Greensville left an indelible impression on his mind. Country songs, with their lonely laments and feeling of quiet despair, moved him. Charles did not consider that style the sole property of white people. Nor did he decide to sing the songs out of rebellion or defiance. He simply loved the music.

He called the album *Modern Sounds in Country and Western Music,* and the first single, "I Can't Stop Loving You," became, to date, the biggest hit of Ray's career, zooming to the top of the R & B and pop charts where it remained number one for months and sold more than 3 million copies. When white actor-singer Tab Hunter put out a version copying Ray's, no one paid much attention to it. It was Ray Charles's interpretation—and his alone—that captivated the country.

Other hits in this style followed: "Born To Lose," "Take These Chains from My Heart," "You Are My Sunshine," "Busted," and "You Don't Know Me." A few critics objected to Charles's use of a white chorus as backup singers instead of the Raeletts, but the public, black fans and white, loved what they heard. Charles's vocal manner did not change on these recordings; he did not try to sound country. Instead, he brought country music to his way of singing. Peter Guralnick, in his 1986 book, *Sweet Soul Music: Rhythm and Blues and the Southern Dream of Freedom,* wrote that Charles's change in direction was "a typically contrary Ray Charles move, one in which he challenged record company, fans, trends, and musical conventions only to come up with a new racially mixed audience of hitherto undreamt-of proportions." Ironically, as a black artist, Ray Charles did more to open up country-and-western music to a general audience than any white artist had done previously. ABC released the second volume of *Modern Sounds in Country and Western Music* in 1963.

By singing songs he had long admired, Ray Charles pulled off the biggest crossover move of his life. In 1962 and 1963, before the advent of the British pop group the Beatles and the rise of the Motown sound, Ray Charles was the most popular singer in the United States. In 1963, he bought a two-storied office building in Los Angeles and custom-built his own studio. Within a short time he learned the complex workings of the studio equipment. He could, and often did, engineer his own records. Ray, Della, and their three sons moved into a beautiful house, which Della helped design, with a swimming pool, in an upper-middle-class black neighborhood only 15 minutes away from Ray's office building. Ray Charles seemed to have everything. Then, in 1964, his world came to a crashing halt.

In a scene from Ballad in Blue, *a film produced in England in 1964, Ray (who plays himself) and the blind boy he befriends in the movie drive a bumper car. Charles enjoyed acting in the movie, which told of a blind boy's quest for confidence and independence.*

7

FREE AT LAST

ALWAYS A WORKAHOLIC, Ray Charles never stopped touring and recording, not for a single month since he had started in the music business as a teenager. In 1964, he went to England and Ireland to star in a movie, called *Ballad in Blue,* and even wrote the title song. (In the United States, the movie was entitled *Blues for Lovers.*) In the Warner Brothers picture, Ray plays himself and befriends a blind boy who is overprotected by his mother. Charles persuades the boy's mother to allow her son to be more independent. Ray enjoyed working on the film, even though it was not a box office hit.

Each year Ray Charles had turned out at least one album, sometimes two. In the early 1960s, with the advent of tracking, a technique that records instruments on separate tracks and allows the vocalist to sing after the music has been made, Charles could indulge his perfectionist instincts. He could go over his vocals as many times as he wanted. In

Ray, with an alto saxophone, appears with his big band in the early 1960s.

fact, he had the power to do anything he wanted—and this turned out to be to work, to perform, and to get high.

It was the getting high that got Charles busted for the third time. It happened in the winter of 1964 at Boston's Logan Airport when he was returning from Canada. In the pockets of the overcoat he carried he had marijuana and heroin. Someone of Charles's stature could have had an assistant carry the coat or hold the drugs or him, but that was not Ray Charles's way. If he was doing something illegal, he wanted to take the blame if he got caught. Charles's bust made headlines throughout the world.

It would take a year of hearings before he was to be sentenced by the judge. The year 1965 turned out to be one of the most critical of his life. For the first time in his career, he decided to take a break from touring. He needed to sort things out for himself, to think about the consequences of going to prison. He considered his children and their reaction to the fact that their father would be called a junkie or a jailbird. Concluding that he had been indulging himself for too long, Charles decided to kick his drug habit. One August morning he walked into the office of Joe Adams, his manager, and explained his decision plainly. "I'm checking into a hospital," he said, "and I'm kicking heroin."

The hospital he admitted himself into was St. Francis in Lynwood, California, just outside of Los Angeles. The doctors offered to wean Ray off heroin gradually, but he refused their offer. Instead of stopping little by little, his approach was to go cold turkey, to just quit. According to Charles, it took the poison some 96 hours to be expelled from his body. "I vomited and vomited until there was nothing left to vomit," he recalled. "And then I vomited some more. I was heaving up poison. The poison which was heroin, the poison my body was naturally rejecting. And it was bitter—bitter as gall. You can't imagine how bitter bitter can be. I was nauseated for days. My body stunk. My sweat stunk. Everything about me stunk." The cold turkey method worked. He gave up heroin for good.

While in the hospital, Charles combated his restlessness by learning chess, feeling the position of the pieces and keeping the layout of the board in his mind at all times. He became an excellent player and lifelong devotee of the game.

Charles's lawyers visited him in the hospital to discuss his upcoming sentencing in Boston. They thought they could gain leniency for him if he would name a few drug pushers. He refused. Ray claimed that the pushers never sought him out; he sought *them* out and refused to blame or accuse anyone of anything. After all, it was his own decision to take drugs, and he alone would pay the price for his wrongdoing.

Charles was released from the hospital in early winter 1965 and shortly thereafter flew to Boston to face the judge. He did not testify. He had already pleaded guilty and had nothing more to add to his statement. Charles's doctor testified that Ray had given up heroin and presented official reports about his patient's physical condition. Ray was understandably nervous under the circumstances— the judge had the power to send him to jail for years.

After hearing the evidence, the court decided to postpone Charles's sentencing for another year. Meanwhile, Charles was assigned a parole officer and could be medically examined without prior notice at any given time to make sure he had not gone back to using heroin. He was pleased about the delay because it meant that he could leave the courtroom, carry on with his life, and, at least for the moment, avoid prison.

Still weary from his ordeal, Charles decided to take off the rest of the year. He needed more time to recuperate, to keep his mind clear and his thoughts focused. Twelve months later, when his probation period ended and he returned to Boston, he learned that the original judge for his case had died just two weeks earlier and a new judge,

Ray and his manager, Joe Adams (center), are photographed before a concert in the mid-1960s. After Ray's drug bust in Boston in the winter of 1964, he walked into Adams's office one morning and said, "I'm checking into a hospital and I'm kicking heroin."

one with a reputation as a tough enforcer, had taken his place. Charles became very anxious about the outcome of his case.

Once again, Ray Charles's doctor testified on his behalf, explaining that Charles was still free of heroin. Periodic

checkups had shown he was not using any drugs. During the testimony, the stern judge was handed a letter in a sealed envelope. The letter had been written by the previous judge while on his deathbed. The courtroom remained silent as the correspondence was read aloud: "I know this

On March 29, 1965, the Reverend Martin Luther King, Jr. (foreground, center), leads the Selma-to-Montgomery (Alabama) civil rights march. Charles, who over the years experienced segregation and discrimination firsthand, admired King and supported the civil rights cause by playing benefit concerts whenever possible.

case is no longer in my jurisdiction, but I believe—as a fellow human being—that society would be better off with Ray Charles free, serving as a good example of a man who has kicked drugs."

The current judge was impressed by all that he had heard during the proceedings. He handed down a five-year probated sentence. Ray Charles left the courtroom a free man.

Charles was concerned, however, about the attitude the public might have about his personal problems. Articles about his predicament had appeared in newspapers and magazines throughout the world. Would his fans accept him back? How would they react?

In spite of the publicity about his drug busts—or perhaps because of it—attendance at his concerts was larger than ever. When Charles returned to the music scene, his fans were there for him. In 1966, he enjoyed great success with "Crying Time," another song in the country-and-western style. He toured the world, recorded a number of movie themes, including "In the Heat of the Night" for Quincy Jones, and he also recorded classic versions of the Beatles' songs "Eleanor Rigby" and "Yesterday."

Throughout the 1960s Charles became politically active. He was a close friend of Martin Luther King, Jr.'s and later explained his support of King and the civil rights cause:

> From the start I had respect for Martin. He reminded me of Jackie Robinson. Same kind of situation. These were the first cats to break down barriers made of iron and steel. Both guys took punishment and abuse for a whole race of people. . . . And then Martin said something which closed the deal for me: "I'll be on the front line, right there next to you." . . . What Martin was telling you to do, he was doing himself. . . . He saw the black struggle in America in worldwide terms, and I liked that thought. He exposed [America's] hypocrisy and [its] injustices for everyone to see. If we were judging the rest of the world, let the rest of the world judge us.

Instead of joining protests and marches, however, Charles chose to work behind the scenes, playing benefits and contributing both his time and money to the civil rights movement.

In the 1970s, Charles and his sons David (left) and Ray junior attend an awards banquet, where Ray is named Man of the Year by the Beverly Hills, California, chapter of B'nai B'rith (the oldest and largest Jewish service organization in the United States).

8

THE LEGEND

DEDICATING HIMSELF TO MUSIC for more than 45 years, Ray
Charles has become a cultural institution, one of the most recognized
and respected artists in the world. Although his records do not sell as
well as they did in the 1960s, he has realized a number of creative
triumphs since then.

In 1972, Charles recorded a gospel-tinged version of "America, the
Beautiful" that became a classic on his ABC album *A Message from
the People*. A year later, Charles left ABC to form his own label,
Crossover, recording not only his own music but also producing artists
he had long admired, including Louis Jordan, Percy Mayfield, and
Little Jimmy Scott. (Tangerine, a recording company Charles had
created in 1968, was renamed Crossover in 1973.) Meanwhile, an
entire generation of singers modeled themselves after his style and
achieved unprecedented success. His disciples included Englishmen

Dan Aykroyd (left), Ray Charles, and John Belushi appear in a scene from the 1980 film The Blues Brothers. *Ray played the role of a music store owner who bargains with the Blues Brothers over instruments.*

Joe Cocker, Rod Stewart, and Steve Winwood, and virtually everyone entering the arena of rock and roll and rhythm and blues at the time.

In 1971, Ray Charles's duet with Aretha Franklin on "Spirit in the Dark," recorded live at the Fillmore West Theater in San Francisco, electrified the hippie generation. Five years later, his interpretation of George Gershwin's *Porgy and Bess,* recorded on two albums and sung with Cleo Laine, pleased the over-40 crowd. Musically, Charles had become all things to all people. "People," he once commented, "have come up to me and said, 'Thank you for introducing me to jazz.' Then someone else will say, 'Thanks for turning me on to blues.' Another fan will tell me I'm the one who got them into country music. Everybody sees me in a different way, but I see myself as a utility player. I like to think I can play all the positions."

Charles re-signed with Atlantic in 1977. He then moved to Columbia for another series of country records, including a collaboration with Willie Nelson, entitled "Seven Spanish Angels," which became a hit. In the early 1990s he began to record for Warner, which in 1993 released *My World*.

The walls of Charles's large Los Angeles office are lined with awards and trophies, far too many to mention here. To date he has received 10 Grammy awards from the recording industry, including the Grammy Lifetime Achievement Award in 1988. When Ray Charles was asked which awards mean the most to him, he replied, "When the Georgia legislature made my version of 'Georgia on My Mind' the official state song in 1979, they invited me to the capitol to sing it in the House of Representatives. That touched my heart. I cried. Then in 1986 I was one of the Kennedy Center honorees. They put the thing on national television and there was President

On December 7, 1986, Ray Charles was honored, along with six other eminent Americans, at the John F. Kennedy Center for the Performing Arts in Washington, D.C., for his contributions to American performing arts.

Reagan, the most powerful cat in the world, hanging this medal around my neck. The hip part was sitting up there in the box watching people entertain *me*."

Other highlights include: the 1978 publication of his autobiography, entitled *Brother Ray;* his inauguration as one of the original inductees in the Rock and Roll Hall of Fame in New York City in 1986; his cameo appearance in the 1980 film *The Blues Brothers,* which starred Dan Aykroyd and John Belushi; his leading the final chorus on the 1985 hit celebrity charity anthem "We Are the World," written by Michael Jackson and Lionel Richie and conducted and produced by Quincy Jones; his video duets with Willie Nelson ("Angel Eyes" in 1984) and Billy Joel ("Baby Grand" in 1986); the PBS/Masters of American Music series documentary *Ray Charles: The Genius of Soul,* originally shown in 1992; the Fox TV tribute celebrating his *Fifty Years of Music Making;* his voice-overs for the claymation California raisins commercials; and his popular television commercials for Diet Pepsi ("You've Got the Right One, Baby, Uh-huh").

On October 7, 1993, President Bill Clinton honored Ray Charles and 17 other eminent Americans at the White House in Washington, D.C., for their contributions to the country's cultural life. While presenting the National Medal of Arts to each of the awardees, Clinton remarked, "These extraordinary individuals have made a gift to American cultural life that is beyond measure. . . . Through these awards we celebrate their impressive achievements and extend our deepest thanks for efforts that nourish our creative and intellectual spirit."

Beginning life as a country boy in Greensville, Florida, Ray Charles found the way, and the courage, to overcome every obstacle that seemed to block his path—the loss of his brother, poverty, blindness, the death of his mother, and drug addiction. Racial discrimination did not stop him from accomplishing his ambitions. Professional rejection did not prevent him from advancing his career. Low-

Ray appeared on the CBS TV program "A Special Kenny Rogers" on December 15, 1981, as Rogers's special guest. Among the other country/pop singers Ray has appeared or recorded with in the past decade are Hank Williams, Jr., Johnny Cash, and Willie Nelson.

On September 20, 1991,
Ray Charles kicks up his heels
while performing "Living in
the City" during the taping
of Ray Charles: 50 Years in
Music, Uh-huh, *a benefit gala
for the Starlight/Starbright
Foundation in Pasadena,
California. Many of the
nation's top R & B, jazz,
rock, pop, and country
musicians later joined the
legendary Charles onstage
in celebrating his half century
of making music.*

paying jobs in dingy clubs, crooked promoters, endless travel down dusty roads . . . nothing stopped him. From the beginning, he has been an individual who has learned to believe in himself.

Ray Charles has risen from the roots of gospel and jazz, shot up the sturdy vine of rhythm and blues and modern soul music—a form many say he invented—spread over the field of country music, and now lords above all these styles as an icon of pure pop, an elder statesman who commands respect from every corner of musical culture, a pioneer, a singularly American phenomenon of endless striving and continued success, a flesh-and-blood emblem of joy's unexpected triumph over pain.

SELECTED DISCOGRAPHY

The following are available on cassette or compact disc:

The Birth of a Legend. Down Beat/Swing Time Recordings, 1949–52.

The Birth of Soul. The Complete Atlantic Rhythm and Blues Recordings, 1952–59.

The Great Ray Charles. Atlantic, 1957.

The Genius of Ray Charles. Atlantic, 1959.

Ray Charles, Live. Atlantic, 1958 Newport Jazz Festival and 1959 Atlanta, Georgia, concert.

Genius Plus Soul Equals Jazz. Sandstone, 1961.

Ray Charles and Betty Carter. Dunhill, 1961.

Modern Sounds in Country and Western Music, Vol. 1. Dunhill, 1962.

Soul Brothers and Soul Meeting, with Milt Jackson. Atlantic, 1962.

Greatest Country and Western Hits. DCC, 1962–63.

His Greatest Hits, Volumes 1 & 2. Dunhill, 1962–63.

Seven Spanish Angels & Other Hits. Sony, 1984.

My World. Warner, 1993.

FURTHER READING

Balliett, Whitney. *American Singers: Twenty-Seven Portraits in Song.* New York: Oxford University Press, 1988.

Charles, Ray, and David Ritz. *Brother Ray: Ray Charles' Own Story.* New York: Da Capo Press, 1992.

Frankl, Ron. *Duke Ellington.* New York: Chelsea House, 1988.

Gillett, Charlie. *Making Tracks: Atlantic Records and the Growth of a Multi-Billion-Dollar Industry.* New York: Dutton, 1974.

————. *The Sound of the City: The Rise of Rock and Roll.* New York: Outerbridge and Dienstfrey, 1970.

Goldberg, Joe. *Jazz Masters of the Fifties.* New York: Macmillan, 1965.

Guralnick, Peter. *Sweet Soul Music: Rhythm and Blues and the Southern Dream of Freedom.* New York: Harper & Row, 1986.

Keil, Charles. *Urban Blues.* Chicago: University of Chicago Press, 1966.

Kliment, Bud. *Count Basie.* New York: Chelsea House, 1992.

Murray, Albert. *Stomping the Blues.* New York: McGraw-Hill, 1976.

Pleasants, Henry. *The Great American Popular Singers.* New York: Simon and Schuster, 1974.

Shaw, Arnold. *Honkers and Shouters: The Golden Years of Rhythm and Blues.* New York: Macmillan, 1978.

Wexler, Jerry, and David Ritz. *Rhythm and the Blues: A Life in American Music.* New York: Knopf, 1993.

CHRONOLOGY

1930	Born Ray Charles Robinson on September 23 in Albany, Georgia; moves with his mother, Aretha, to Greensville, Florida
1935	Is captivated by Wylie Pitman's piano playing at the Red Wing Café; Ray's four-year-old brother, George, accidentally drowns; Ray begins to gradually lose his eyesight from glaucoma
1937	In September is sent to board at the Florida State School for the Deaf and the Blind, located in St. Augustine; learns to read and write braille
1938	Has right eye extracted after it becomes infected; learns to read and write music in braille at school and studies classical music
1940	Plays piano and sings for black ladies' tea parties
1945	In May, Aretha Robinson dies of a heart attack at age 32; Ray leaves school and begins his career as a musician, working in the Florida cities of Jacksonville, Orlando, and Tampa; meets Louise
1948	Plays piano with the Florida Playboys, a white hillbilly band; moves to Seattle, Washington; forms the McSon Trio; begins using illegal drugs
1949	Meets Jack Lauderdale of Down Beat Records (later called Swing Time); writes and records his first minor hit, "Baby, Let Me Hold Your Hand"
1950	Moves to Los Angeles, California; Louise gives birth to Ray's daughter, Evelyn; tours with Lowell Fulson's band
1951	Marries Eileen; leaves Fulson's band and performs solo
1952	Signs with Shaw Agency; switches from Swing Time label to Atlantic Records in New York City
1953	Divorces Eileen; assembles his first band in Dallas, Texas
1954	Writes "I Got a Woman," his first gospel-blues song
1955	Marries Della; tours as backup singer for Ruth Brown; takes charge of his recording sessions at Atlantic
1956	Della gives birth to a son, Ray junior
1957	Adds female backup singers, the Raeletts, to his ensemble
1958	Performs at Newport Jazz Festival; records *Soul Brothers* with Milt Jackson; arrested for drug possession in Philadelphia, Pennsylvania;

Della gives birth to a second son, David; the Charles family moves to Los Angeles, California

1959 Records his first Top 10 crossover hit, "What I Say"; performs at New York City's Carnegie Hall; releases *The Genius of Ray Charles*; signs with ABC Records; the Raelett Margie Hendrix gives birth to Ray's son Charles Wayne

1960 Releases his first number one crossover hit, "Georgia on My Mind"; Charles and his octet travel to Europe for the first time

1961 Is arrested on drug charges in Indianapolis, Indiana; releases *Genius Plus Soul Equals Jazz*; puts together a big band; Della gives birth to a third son, Bobby

1962 Begins his country-and-western recordings with *Modern Sounds in Country and Western Music*

1963 Buys office building in Los Angeles and builds a recording studio

1964 Travels to England and Ireland to film *Ballad in Blue*; in winter is arrested for possession of heroin at Boston's Logan Airport

1965 Goes through rehabilitation; decides not to tour; in August is admitted to a Lynwood, California, hospital to kick drug habit

1966 Receives a five-year probated sentence from the Boston judge; releases "Crying Time"

1973 Ends his association with ABC Records and releases his recordings on his own label, Crossover

1975 Marriage to Della ends in divorce

1977 Re-signs with Atlantic for the marketing and distribution of his records

1983 Switches to the country division of Columbia Records

1986 Is honored by President Ronald Reagan with a Kennedy Center Award, presented during a nationally televised program in Washington, D.C.; inducted into the Rock and Roll Hall of Fame

1991 Leaves Columbia Records and joins Warner Bros.

1993 Releases *My World*; is awarded a National Medal of Arts by President Bill Clinton at the White House on October 7

INDEX

David Ritz is the author of *Divided Soul: The Life of Marvin Gaye* and coauthor of the autobiographies of Ray Charles, Smokey Robinson, and Jerry Wexler. His novels include *Family Blood* and *Passion Flowers*. Ritz lives in Los Angeles, California.

ACKNOWLEDGMENTS
The author wishes to thank his wife, Roberta, for her editorial help and inspiration.

Jerry Lewis is the National Chairman of the Muscular Dystrophy Association (MDA) and host of the MDA Labor Day Telethon. An internationally acclaimed comedian, Lewis began his entertainment career in New York and then performed in a comedy team with singer and actor Dean Martin from 1946 to 1956. Lewis has appeared in many films—including *The Delicate Delinquent, Rock a Bye Baby, The Bellboy, Cinderfella, The Nutty Professor, The Disorderly Orderly,* and *The King of Comedy*—and his comedy performances continue to delight audiences around the world.

John Callahan is a nationally syndicated cartoonist and the author of an illustrated autobiography, *Don't Worry, He Won't Get Far on Foot.* He has also produced three cartoon collections: *Do Not Disturb Any Further, Digesting the Child Within,* and *Do What He Says! He's Crazy!!!* He has recently been the subject of feature articles in the *New York Times Magazine,* the *Los Angeles Times Magazine,* and the Cleveland *Plain Dealer,* and has been profiled on "60 Minutes." Callahan resides in Portland, Oregon.